Edexcel GCSE (9-1)
History

British America, 1713–1783: empire and revolution

Series Editor: Angela Leonard   Author: Simon Davis

ALWAYS LEARNING

Published by Pearson Education Limited, 80 Strand, London WC2R 0RL.

www.pearsonschoolsandfecolleges.co.uk

Copies of official specifications for all Edexcel qualifications may be found on the website: www.edexcel.com

Text © Pearson Education Limited 2016

Series editor: Angela Leonard
Designed by Colin Tilley Loughrey, Pearson Education Limited
Typeset by Phoenix Photosetting, Chatham, Kent
Original illustrations © Pearson Education Limited
Illustrated by KJA Artists Illustration Agency and Phoenix Photosetting, Chatham, Kent.

Cover design by Colin Tilley Loughrey
Picture research by Christine Martin
Cover photo © Bridgeman Art Library Ltd: Sterling and Francine Clark Art Institute, Williamstown, Massachusetts, USA.

The right of Simon Davis to be identified as author of this work has been asserted by him in accordance with the Copyright, Designs and Patents Act 1988.

First published 2016

19 18 17
10 9 8 7 6 5 4 3

British Library Cataloguing in Publication Data
A catalogue record for this book is available from the British Library.
ISBN 978 1 292 12729 3

Printed in Slovakia by Neografia

A note from the publisher
In order to ensure that this resource offers high-quality support for the associated Pearson qualification, it has been through a review process by the awarding body. This process confirms that this resource fully covers the teaching and learning content of the specification or part of a specification at which it is aimed. It also confirms that it demonstrates an appropriate balance between the development of subject skills, knowledge and understanding, in addition to preparation for assessment.

Endorsement does not cover any guidance on assessment activities or processes (e.g. practice questions or advice on how to answer assessment questions), included in the resource nor does it prescribe any particular approach to the teaching or delivery of a related course.

While the publishers have made every attempt to ensure that advice on the qualification and its assessment is accurate, the official specification and associated assessment guidance materials are the only authoritative source of information and should always be referred to for definitive guidance.

Pearson examiners have not contributed to any sections in this resource relevant to examination papers for which they have responsibility.

Examiners will not use endorsed resources as a source of material for any assessment set by Pearson.

Endorsement of a resource does not mean that the resource is required to achieve this Pearson qualification, nor does it mean that it is the only suitable material available to support the qualification, and any resource lists produced by the awarding body shall include this and other appropriate resources.

Websites
Pearson Education Limited is not responsible for the content of any external Internet sites. It is essential for tutors to preview each website before using it in class so as to ensure that the URL is still accurate, relevant and appropriate. We suggest that tutors bookmark useful websites and consider enabling students to access them through the school/college intranet.

Contents

How to use this book

What's covered?

This book covers the Period Study on British America, 1713–83. This unit makes up 20% of your GCSE course, and will be examined in Paper 2.

Period studies cover a specific period of time of around 50 years, and require you to know about and be able to analyse the events surrounding important developments and issues that happened in this period. You need to understand how the different topics covered fit into the overall narrative. This book also explains the different types of exam questions you will need to answer, and includes advice and example answers to help you improve.

Features

As well as a clear, detailed explanation of the key knowledge you will need, you will also find a number of features in the book:

Key terms

Where you see a word followed by an asterisk, like this: Proclamation*, you will be able to find a Key terms box on that page that explains what the word means.

> **Key term**
>
> Proclamation*
> An official announcement.

Activities

Every few pages, you'll find a box containing some activities designed to help check and embed knowledge and get you to really think about what you've studied. The activities start simple, but might get more challenging as you work through them.

Summaries and Checkpoints

At the end of each chunk of learning, the main points are summarised in a series of bullet points – great for embedding the core knowledge, and handy for revision.

Checkpoints help you to check and reflect on your learning. The Strengthen section helps you to consolidate knowledge and understanding, and check that you've grasped the basic ideas and skills. The Challenge questions push you to go beyond just understanding the information, and into evaluation and analysis of what you've studied.

Sources and Interpretations

Although source work and interpretations do not appear in Paper 2, you'll still find interesting contemporary material throughout the books, showing what people from the period said, thought or created, helping you to build your understanding of people in the past.

The book also includes extracts from the work of historians, showing how experts have interpreted the events you've been studying.

> **Source E**
>
> Benjamin West's painting, *Franklin Drawing Electricity from the Sky* (1805). Although not an accurate representation, it shows Franklin's experiment that lightning had electrical properties.

> **Interpretation 1**
>
> An extract from the book *The American Pageant* by David Kennedy, Lizabeth Cohen and Thomas Bailey, published in 2002. It explores the significance of the Great Awakening and suggests that it united the American colonists, which is an idea that historians debate.
>
> The Awakening left many lasting effects. Its emphasis on direct, emotive spirituality seriously undermined the older clergy [ministers], whose authority had derived from their education… [It] greatly increased the numbers and the competitiveness of American churches. It encouraged a fresh wave of missionary work among the Indians and even among black slaves, many of whom also attended the mass open-air revivals. It led to the founding of 'new light' centers of higher learning such as Princeton, Brown, Rutgers, and Dartmouth. Perhaps most significant, the Great Awakening was the first spontaneous mass movement of the American people. It tended to break down… boundaries… and contributed to the growing sense that Americans had of themselves as a single people, united by a common history and shared experiences.

Extend your knowledge

These features contain useful additional information that adds depth to your knowledge, and to your answers. The information is closely related to the key issues in the unit, and questions are sometimes included, helping you to link the new details to the main content.

> **Extend your knowledge**
>
> **The Quok Walker case, 1781**
> A slave called Quok Walker took part in the first court case to free a slave in Massachusetts. In 1781, Walker ran away from his master, Nathaniel Jennison, to work for a neighbour. When Jennison tried to sue his neighbour, Walker countersued. Jennison lost the case because of the 'born free' clause in the constitution of Massachusetts, and Walker gained his freedom.
>
> How strong is the link between the Quok Walker case and the Declaration of Independence?

Exam-style questions and tips

The book also includes extra exam-style questions you can use to practise. These appear in the chapters and are accompanied by a tip to help you get started on an answer.

Exam-style question, Section A

Write a narrative account analysing the key events of 1758–60 that led to the French surrender.

You may use the following in your answer:

- the French abandon Fort Duquesne (1758)
- the capture of Montreal (1760).

You **must** also use information of your own.   **8 marks**

Exam tip

This question targets your ability to write an analytical narrative. In your answer, consider the links between each event in the lead-up to the capture of Montreal.

Recap pages

At the end of each chapter, you'll find a page designed to help you to consolidate and reflect on the chapter as a whole. Each recap page includes a recall quiz, ideal for quickly checking your knowledge or for revision. Recap pages also include activities designed to help you summarise and analyse what you've learned, and also reflect on how each chapter links to other parts of the unit.

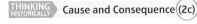
THINKING HISTORICALLY

These activities are designed to help you develop a better understanding of how history is constructed, and are focused on the key areas of Evidence, Interpretations, Cause & Consequence and Change & Continuity. In the Period Study, you will come across an activity on Cause & Consequence, as this is a key focus for this unit.

The Thinking Historically approach has been developed in conjunction with Dr Arthur Chapman and the Institute of Education, UCL. It is based on research into the misconceptions that can hold students back in history.

THINKING HISTORICALLY ▸ Cause and Consequence (2c) ─── conceptual map reference

The Thinking Historically conceptual map can be found at: www.pearsonschools.co.uk/thinkinghistoricallygcse

WRITING HISTORICALLY

At the end of most chapters is a spread dedicated to helping you improve your writing skills. These include simple techniques you can use in your writing to make your answers clearer, more precise and better focused on the question you're answering.

The Writing Historically approach is based on the *Grammar for Writing* pedagogy developed by a team at the University of Exeter and popular in many English departments. Each spread uses examples from the preceding chapter, so it's relevant to what you've just been studying.

Preparing for your exams

At the back of the book, you'll find a special section dedicated to explaining and exemplifying the new Edexcel GCSE History exams. Advice on the demands of this paper, written by Angela Leonard, helps you prepare for and approach the exam with confidence. Each question type is explained through annotated sample answers at two levels, showing clearly how answers can be improved.

Pearson Progression Scale: This icon indicates the Step that a sample answer has been graded at on the Pearson Progression Scale.

This book is also available as an online ActiveBook, which can be licensed for your whole institution.

There is also an ActiveLearn Digital Service available to support delivery of this book, featuring a front-of-class version of the book, lesson plans, worksheets, exam practice PowerPoints, assessments, notes on Thinking Historically and Writing Historically, and more.

ActiveLearn
Digital Service

Timeline: British America, 1713–83

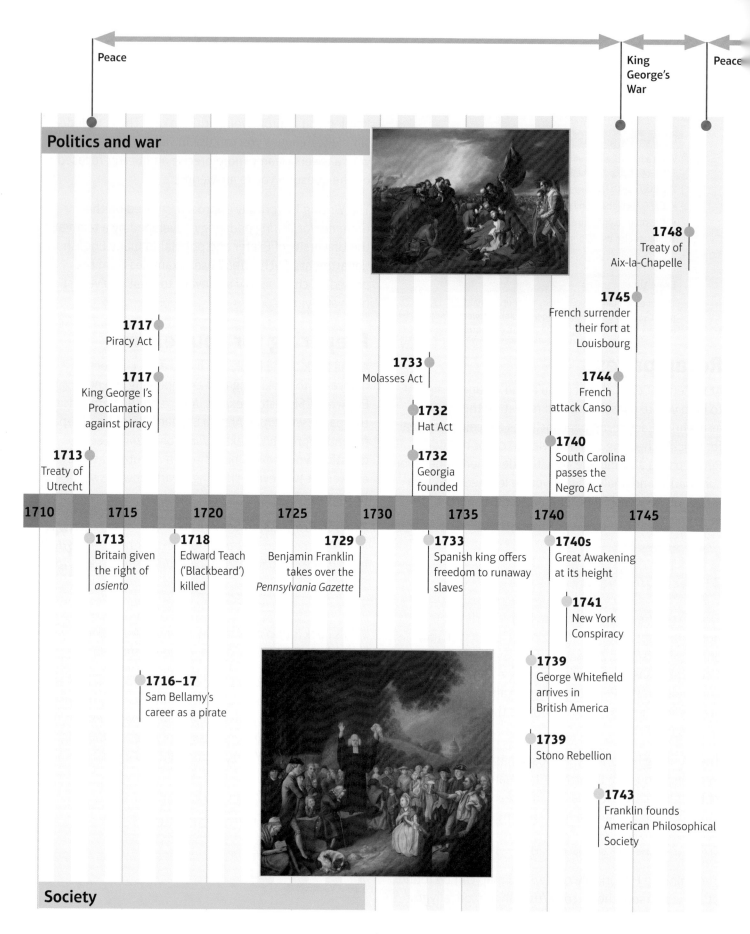

Peace

King George's War

Peace

Politics and war

1748
Treaty of Aix-la-Chapelle

1745
French surrender their fort at Louisbourg

1744
French attack Canso

1740
South Carolina passes the Negro Act

1717
Piracy Act

1717
King George I's Proclamation against piracy

1733
Molasses Act

1732
Hat Act

1732
Georgia founded

1713
Treaty of Utrecht

1710   1715   1720   1725   1730   1735   1740   1745

1713
Britain given the right of *asiento*

1718
Edward Teach ('Blackbeard') killed

1729
Benjamin Franklin takes over the *Pennsylvania Gazette*

1733
Spanish king offers freedom to runaway slaves

1740s
Great Awakening at its height

1741
New York Conspiracy

1739
George Whitefield arrives in British America

1716–17
Sam Bellamy's career as a pirate

1739
Stono Rebellion

1743
Franklin founds American Philosophical Society

Society

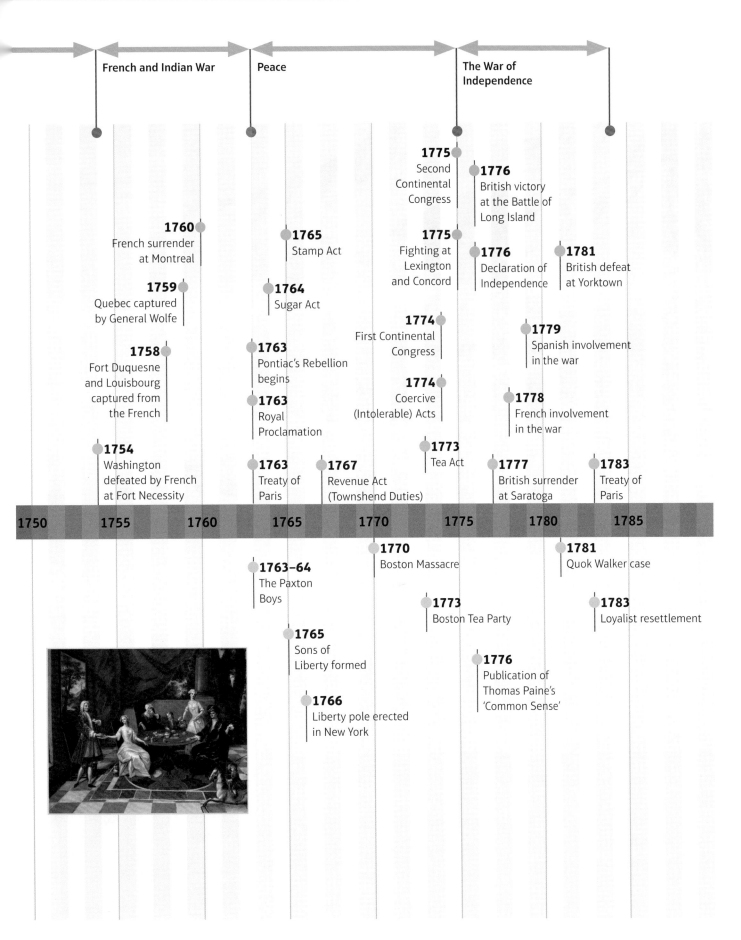

French and Indian War

Peace

The War of
Independence

1775
Second
Continental
Congress

1776
British victory
at the Battle of
Long Island

1760
French surrender
at Montreal

1765
Stamp Act

1775
Fighting at
Lexington
and Concord

1776
Declaration of
Independence

1781
British defeat
at Yorktown

1759
Quebec captured
by General Wolfe

1764
Sugar Act

1774
First Continental
Congress

1779
Spanish involvement
in the war

1758
Fort Duquesne
and Louisbourg
captured from
the French

1763
Pontiac's Rebellion
begins

1774
Coercive
(Intolerable) Acts

1778
French involvement
in the war

1763
Royal
Proclamation

1773
Tea Act

1754
Washington
defeated by French
at Fort Necessity

1763
Treaty of
Paris

1767
Revenue Act
(Townshend Duties)

1777
British surrender
at Saratoga

1783
Treaty of
Paris

1750	1755	1760	1765	1770	1775	1780	1785

1770
Boston Massacre

1781
Quok Walker case

1763–64
The Paxton
Boys

1773
Boston Tea Party

1783
Loyalist resettlement

1765
Sons of
Liberty formed

1776
Publication of
Thomas Paine's
'Common Sense'

1766
Liberty pole erected
in New York

01 | British settlement in North America, 1713–41

When Blackbeard took charge of his first pirate ship in 1716, his prospects looked good. British America was full of riches, which were his for the taking. A few years later, he and his fellow captains were caught and killed. They had enjoyed brief success, but nothing more. In contrast, when thousands of German migrants arrived in America with their families in tow, they had a chance to break out of overpopulated Europe and set up their own farms. Many enjoyed long-term prosperity. However, this prosperity wasn't shared by the many Africans who were forced to cross the Atlantic in the 18th century. These men and women were a key reason the economy of British America thrived, but they were treated poorly and sometimes driven to revolt.

Their experience differed hugely to that of the leaders of colonial society, made up of men and women who had gone to British America to exercise power and build up their reputation. In one way, they lived a life of luxury, enjoying a similar experience to the gentry back in Britain. In another, they lived a life forever at risk from slave rebellion, and they faced the challenge of controlling a small but troublesome population of smugglers, pirates and land-hungry migrants.

Learning outcomes

By the end of this chapter, you will understand:

* the impact of expansion, immigration, economic developments and piracy on colonial society
* the significance of the slave trade and slavery for the economy and society of British America
* the effects of rebellion, conspiracy and smuggling on British America.

1.1 Developments in colonial society

British America in 1713

In 1713, over one hundred years had passed since the first English colony* had been established in America. By this time, Britain controlled a strip of land along the eastern coast of North America, bordered by Canada to the north and Florida to the south.

The settlers who had gone to live there were a mixed bunch, including wealthy landowners, poor servants and slaves*. Some went through choice, as they were attracted by the huge amounts of land available in America. Others were pushed by circumstance – they could not find a job or were persecuted for their religious beliefs in Britain. Many were even forced to go, taken from their home country in order to work in the American colonies as slaves.

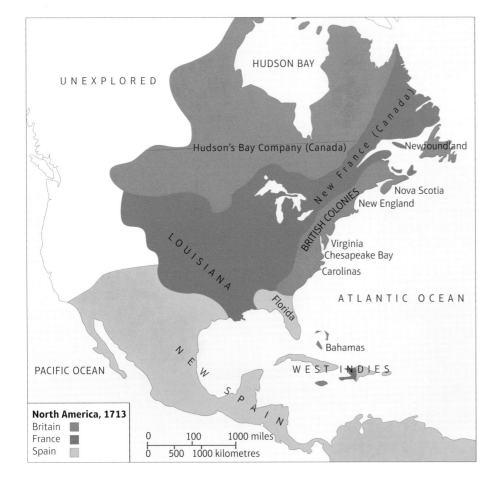

Key terms

Colony*

A country or area that is part of an empire. Britain was called the mother country and North America contained some of its colonies.

Slaves*

People who have become the property of a master and are made to work without pay. Most slaves were forcibly taken from their homes in West Africa to work in the colonies.

Figure 1.1 A map of North America in 1713. It shows the areas controlled by Britain, France and Spain.

The British settlers were not alone. They were surrounded by enemies who wanted their land. The French threatened them from the north and west, the Spanish from the south. Native Americans lived in or along the entire British land border. This competition for land was why, in 1713, the colonists had just emerged from 12 years of war with the French and Spanish, ended by the Treaty of Utrecht, and continued to live in constant fear of Native American raids.

Pattern of settlement: the British colonies in 1713

A settler arriving in the middle colonies of British America in 1713 would see a very different picture to a settler who travelled to the north or the south. Figure 1.2 summarises what they might have seen.

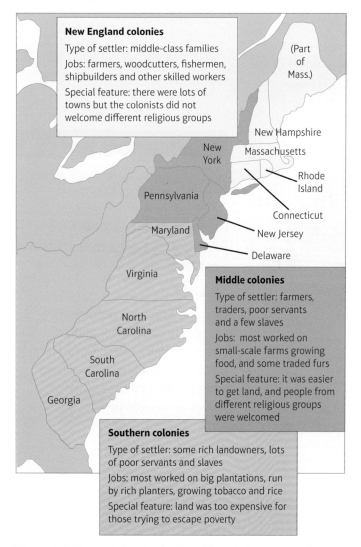

Figure 1.2 The mainland colonies of British America in the early 18th century.

Government of the colonies

The colonies were a part of the British Empire and all were run by representatives of the British government, as well as a locally elected assembly (see Figure 1.3).

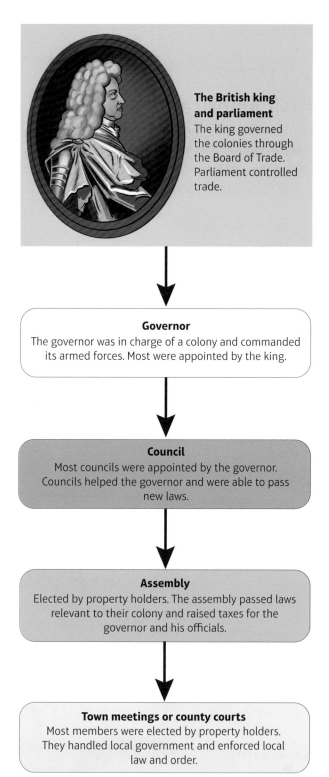

Figure 1.3 The government of the colonies.

Impact of expansion of the colonies and immigration

Expansion

The colonies had a high rate of natural increase*. In Europe, the average rate of natural increase was 1%, but in British America the average was around 3%. This meant that the population grew rapidly. The borders of British America began to expand, as colonists travelled to the west and south in search of land. As a result, between 1701 and 1750, one new colony was established, called Georgia, and 49 new counties* were founded.

Key terms

Natural increase*

The difference between the birth and death rate. If it is a positive figure, then the birth rate is higher than the death rate.

County*

A unit of land with its own local government. A colony was divided into towns and counties.

Immigration

The colonies were a popular destination for a range of immigrant groups in the 1700s, including:

- **Germans**: a large number travelled with their families to North America
- **Scots-Irish**: a big group, made up mainly of young, single people who went as indentured servants*
- **English**: some went if they had family in North America. Convicted criminals were also sent after 1718, when parliament passed a transportation* law.

Key terms

Indentured servants*

People who have signed contracts to work for a fixed number of years, in return for a free journey to the colonies.

Transportation*

A form of punishment in which criminals were sent overseas to work. They usually had to become indentured servants for 14 years.

Extend your knowledge

Georgia

James Oglethorpe founded the colony of Georgia in 1732. It was set up as a charity for poor people who could not afford to emigrate. Settlers received free transport to the colony and a farm when they got there. This led around 1,800 people to settle in Georgia in its first ten years.

Source A

A job reference from Captain Diemer of Pennsylvania for a German immigrant called Gottlieb Mittelberger. It was written in 1750.

Mr Mittelberger has behaved himself honestly, diligently, and faithfully in ye Offices of Schoolmaster and Organist, during ye Space of three Years; in ye Township of New-Providence, County of Philadelphia… So that I and all his Employers were entirely satisfied, and would willingly have him to remain with us. But as… [he wants] to proceed on his long Journey; we would recommend… Mr Mittelberger to all Persons of Dignity and Character.

Activities ?

1. Put yourself in the position of the employer of an indentured servant. You can choose their background. Write a job reference for them, sharing it with the class. Include the following:

   a. Where they had chosen to live. Use Figure 1.2 to help you.

   b. How they ended up in the colonies. Use the information on immigration above to help.

   c. What they did and whether you would recommend them.

2. Discuss in pairs the possible positive and negative effects immigration could have on the British colonies. Record your ideas in a table with columns for 'positive effects' and 'negative effects'.

3. Consider the number of different types of references your class created. Underneath your table, explain whether this variety of backgrounds and trades would make the colonies a better place to live or not.

Consequences of expansion and immigration

Immigrants helped to improve the economy, because they provided a cheap workforce and some had manufacturing skills. They also played an important part in defending the frontier* between the colonists and the Native Americans. However, their arrival had negative consequences, too. It increased competition for land and stirred up tensions.

Colonial expansion and the Native Americans

The Native Americans were unhappy with the expansion of the colonies because immigrants trespassed on their land. For example, many Scots-Irish chose to move to Pennsylvania, but there was not enough land available for them all. Rather than wait for more land to be purchased by the government from the Native Americans, the immigrants settled on Native American territory. The Native Americans were angry with the squatters* and asked for help from the leaders of Pennsylvania, but they refused. Instead of forcing the immigrants off the land that had been stolen, the leaders used their presence to pressure the Native Americans into surrendering it.

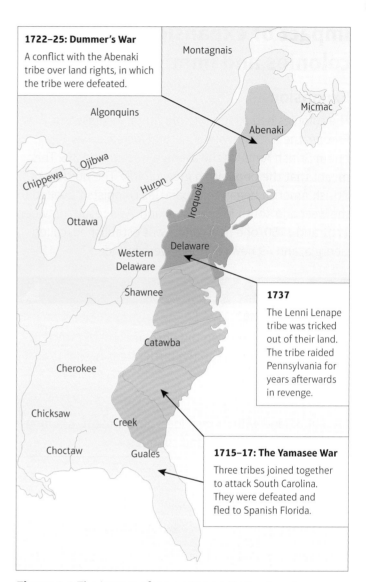

1722–25: Dummer's War
A conflict with the Abenaki tribe over land rights, in which the tribe were defeated.

1737
The Lenni Lenape tribe was tricked out of their land. The tribe raided Pennsylvania for years afterwards in revenge.

1715–17: The Yamasee War
Three tribes joined together to attack South Carolina. They were defeated and fled to Spanish Florida.

Figure 1.4 The impact of expansion on Native American territories.

Key terms
Frontier*
A line or border separating two areas.
Squatters*
People living on land they do not have a legal right to.

A similar pattern of colonial expansion followed by conflict with the Native Americans occurred throughout the colonies. Figure 1.4 illustrates the areas of expansion and some Native American responses.

Immigration and tensions among social groups

A few colonists who had lived in British America for several generations reacted badly to new immigrants. This led to conflict and tension, which took different forms.

- **Tension between religious groups.** Many of the Scots-Irish were Presbyterians*. This upset the people of New England, who were Congregationalists*, and led them to pass an anti-immigration law.

Key terms
Presbyterian*
A form of Protestant Christianity which spread to Scotland during the 16th century. It is highly organised and run by courts, ministers and elders.
Congregationalist*
A follower of Congregationalism. A Congregationalist believes that each church group should be independent, able to elect their own members and should follow a shared set of strict Christian beliefs.

- **Tension between descendants of English settlers and new settlers from mainland Europe.** Some feared that 'foreigners' might swamp their colony. In Pennsylvania, where Germans had become one-third of the population, immigrants were made to swear an oath of loyalty to the colony.

However, in most places the impact was minimal. New immigrants tended to live together, often on the frontier between the established colonies and the Native American lands.

Tensions among other social groups

In addition to immigrants, other social groups competed for power, land and money. Figure 1.5 illustrates the tensions between these groups.

Economic developments
Trade with Britain

About 10% of the goods produced by the colonists was sold to other countries. One of their biggest markets was Britain, because Britain controlled what the colonists could trade and the countries they could trade with. This arrangement might sound like a bad deal for the colonists, but it helped their economy to grow. This was because Britain provided:

- **a market for colonial goods**: it wanted wheat, fish, fur, tobacco and rice
- **consumer goods**: the colonists could buy goods like tea, spices and manufactured clothing
- **cheap manufactured goods**: for example, Britain sold tools that colonists needed to grow crops.

The colonies also received help to improve production:

- **laws** to help industry in the colonies: Britain passed laws to encourage the colonists to build ships to transport their goods
- **finance**: British companies provided insurance and loans to the colonists
- **subsidies**: the British needed certain raw materials, such as indigo*, and gave money to assist production.

Free black colonists | White colonists

There were a small number of free black colonists. In comparison to white colonists, they had few legal rights, faced racist attitudes and were even banned from certain colonies.

Rich landowners and planters | Small farmers and planters | Servants and labourers

Around 50% of white males owned no land. Inequality grew in the 18th century, which created tension between the different ranks in society. For example, rioting took place after the Virginia Inspection Act of 1730 was passed, which disadvantaged small planters in favour of rich landowners.

Rich merchants | Rich landowners

The elites, who ran the colonial government, were divided between two interests:
- **the town:** trading and commerce
- **the countryside:** farming.

There were arguments over which group should pay the most tax and what new laws to support.

Figure 1.5 Tensions among other social groups.

Key term

Indigo*

A plant grown to make a dark blue dye. It was grown in South Carolina from 1741.

Source B

An image of Boston Harbor from the 1700s. It shows some of the different products that were sent to Britain from the New England colonies.

Trade with the West Indies

Another consequence of being part of the British Empire was that the North American colonies were encouraged to trade with other British colonies. These included some of the islands in the West Indies, parts of Canada, and Newfoundland (see Figure 1.1).

In 1733, the British government introduced the Molasses* Act, which strengthened trade with the West Indies (see page 32). The North American colonists sold food supplies to the West Indies and bought molasses in return. Molasses could be turned into rum, which became a valuable consumer product in the colonies.

Key term

Molasses*

The juice that is produced when raw sugar is processed on a plantation.

The importance of tobacco

Tobacco was grown in some of the southern colonies and was very important to their economies. It made up about 45% of everything British America sold to other countries. There was high demand for it in Britain, which meant the colonists could charge high prices. As a result, some southerners grew very wealthy.

However, there were negative effects of relying so much on the sale of tobacco. The colonists put themselves at risk if there was a drop in demand, or too much was produced, because the sale price would drop. When this happened in the 1720s and early 1730s, the income of tobacco planters fell.

The introduction of tea

In the 1700s, coffee was replaced by tea as the most fashionable drink. It was brought into Britain from India, which was also a part of the British Empire, and some of it was then resold to British America. Tea made up around 12% of the products that went through Britain on their way to the colonies. This helped to spread the social habits of the mother country to its colonies.

Source C

A British family taking tea, painted by Gavin Hamilton, a Scottish-born painter, in the 1750s.

At first, tea became very important in sophisticated female society in the colonies. Wealthy women would hold tea parties in special rooms designed for drinking tea. However, by the middle of the 18th century, it was popular with everyone from rich to poor. This strengthened their bond with Britain, where drinking tea had also become a feature of everyday life.

Source D

A New Yorker reported on how important tea was to colonial life in 1734.

I am credibly informed that tea and china ware cost the province, yearly, near the sum of £10,000; and people that are least able to go to the expence, must have tea [even] tho' their families want bread... I am told they often pawn their rings and plate to gratifie themselves in that piece of extravagance.

Activity ?

Look at Sources C and D. Imagine you plan to send the painting in Source C as a gift to a New Yorker in the 1700s. Write the gift tag you would send with it. You should explain why you chose that painting.

The impact of piracy

The years 1715 to 1725 are called the golden age of piracy, because this was the time when pirate* fleets roamed the Bahamas and the coves of the Carolinas. At the beginning of this period, there were around 2,000 pirates who preyed on merchant ships*.

Their presence had three main effects.

- **Trade goods were lost**: over 2,400 ships were captured or destroyed by pirates in this period.
- **The cost of trading went up**: insurance prices grew rapidly as a result of losses.
- **They created fear**: people were afraid to travel in case they were killed or forced to join the pirates.

Key terms

Pirate*

A sailor who attacks and steals from other ships.

Merchant ships*

Ships that transported goods and passengers for profit.

The impact of 'Black Sam' Bellamy's activities

Sam Bellamy began his career in piracy in 1716. He had formed a partnership with Paulsgrave Williams, who gave him the money he needed to recruit a crew and buy two periaguas*. A few months later, he impressed another pirate captain, Benjamin Hornigold, when he stole a prize ship from one of Hornigold's enemies. Hornigold gave Bellamy his first pirate ship to captain: the *Marianne*.

Key term

Periagua*

A large wooden boat that looks like a canoe, which can carry around 30 people.

From then on, Bellamy went from strength to strength. He built up a crew of 170 pirates and, by early 1717, had managed to capture a galley ship*. This ship, called the *Whydah*, had enough cannon and speed to attack a warship of the Royal Navy. Its first voyage, which began in March 1717, had a big impact. It stopped much of the trade in the Chesapeake Bay area.

However, Bellamy's terrifying voyage was cut short in May 1717, when a heavy storm destroyed the *Whydah* and killed Bellamy. His time sailing between the West Indies to Massachusetts had come to an end. In that time, he had damaged trade, created fear and caused the loss of over 50 ships.

Key term

Galley*

A ship powered by rowing, or using a sail. The *Whydah* had three masts for sailing, but also had space for oarsmen.

Source E

An extract from a conversation between Sam Bellamy and the captain of a ship he had just captured. Bellamy outlines his justifications for piracy.

Bellamy: 'Damn ye, you are a sneaking puppy, and so are all those who will submit to be governed by laws which rich men have made for their own security... Damn them [as] a pack of crafty Rascals. And you [captains and seamen], who serve them, [as] a parcel of hen-hearted numbskulls! They vilify us, the scoundrels do, when there is only this difference [between us]: they rob the poor under the cover of law... and we plunder the rich under the cover of our own courage.'

The impact of Blackbeard's activities

Edward Teach, also known as Blackbeard, joined Hornigold's crew in 1713. He helped him to attack Spanish trading ships and gained his trust. Three years later, when most of Hornigold's crew had abandoned him, Teach stayed with him and followed him to Nassau. This was a pirate base in the Bahamas, which Teach helped to strengthen. In return for his loyalty, Teach was given his first ship.

Teach's big break came in August 1717, when Stede Bonnet arrived in a ship called the *Revenge*. Bonnet

lacked the skills to command a ship, so Hornigold made Teach its captain. He increased the number of guns on the ship to 12 and increased the crew to 150 men. This gave him the confidence to patrol the coastline of British America in search of riches and prize ships.

His good fortune continued into November, when he captured a French slave ship, which he renamed *Queen Anne's Revenge*. It was similar to Bellamy's ship, the *Whydah*, and was used to attack the surrounding islands and Charleston. Teach built up such a fortune that he decided to abandon many of his crew so that he did not have to share it with them.

Source F

A picture of Edward Teach. It is based on a description of him in a history of piracy written in 1724.

Blackbeard's impact

In July 1718, Teach set himself up with a new home in North Carolina and continued to operate as a pirate until his death in November 1718. In five years, he had made a remarkable impact. He had:

- **captured plunder**: by April 1717, he and Hornigold had captured £100,000 worth of treasure (worth around £13.5 million today)

- **scared the Royal Navy**: during his time with Hornigold in 1717, the Royal Navy ship HMS *Shoreham* was too scared to leave the coastline of Virginia and Maryland
- **attacked merchant shipping**: this affected traders from the Carolinas to New York
- **set up pirate bases**: he helped defend Nassau (1717–18) and made a new home for himself in North Carolina in 1718
- **encouraged some governors to support piracy**: he gained the protection of the governor in North Carolina through bribery.

Activity ?

1. Imagine you have been asked to write the blurb (description) for the back cover of a book about the golden age of piracy. Try to keep your entry under 150 words.
2. Work in pairs. Compare your entries and highlight or label any common themes or ideas you have both used.
3. Create a contents page for the book. It should have five chapters, each with an interesting title. Include the information on the suppression of piracy (see below) as well.

The suppression of piracy in American waters

The British government tried a number of methods to bring piracy to an end. It offered pardons* to those who stopped being a pirate, it strengthened the law against pirates and it sent Royal Navy warships to attack them and take control of their bases. These efforts were supported by some of the colonial governors, who carried out raids against the pirates that patrolled their shores.

Key terms

Pardon*

An official release from the punishment for a crime.

Privateer*

A person who has been authorised to use their own ship to attack and capture enemy ships.

Method 1: King George I's Proclamation

On 5 September 1717, King George I issued a Proclamation* to try to end piracy. He offered:

- A pardon to any pirate, which forgave them for all their crimes as a pirate until January 1718.
- A prize of up to £100 (worth around £13,500 today) for anyone who caught a pirate.

His measure had some success. For example, Captain Pearse of HMS *Phoenix* went to the pirate harbour of Nassau. Around 500 pirates came to him in order to receive a pardon. However, an unintended consequence was that many of these men, including Blackbeard, could not resist the rewards of their old lifestyle and soon returned to piracy.

Key term

Proclamation*

An official announcement.

Exam-style question, Section A

Explain **two** consequences of King George I's Proclamation (1717). **8 marks**

Exam tip

This question is asking you about consequence. Make sure you focus your answer on the actions that the Proclamation led to and the effects it had, rather than the reasons for it.

Method 2: the Piracy Act, 1717

Alongside royal action, parliament took steps to end piracy. The Transportation Act of 1717 contained a section on piracy. It reinforced an earlier law from William III's reign (1689–1702), which described who could put a pirate on trial, how the trial was organised and the penalty for a convicted pirate. Under this Act, a pirate could be put to death.

The law encouraged action against pirates. For example, in 1718, Woodes Rodgers, a former privateer* and the owner of a merchant shipping company, assembled a fleet of seven ships, which included two from the Royal Navy. They sailed to Nassau so that he could take control as governor. By December 1718, he had begun to restore order and put any remaining pirates on trial.

Another effect of the Piracy Act was an increase in the number of pirates who were captured, tried and executed. In 1718, 110 pirates were hanged and, by 1726, around 600 had been executed. This was mainly due to the actions of Royal Navy warship captains, merchant ship captains and local governors.

Case study: the work of Governor Spotswood

Alexander Spotswood was the governor of Virginia. He took direct action to reduce the number of pirates.

- **He asked for help**: in 1714 he told the British Board of Trade* that piracy had become common on the shores of Virginia.
- **He took legal action**: when one of Teach's officers was captured, Spotswood ensured his trial did not involve a jury. He was worried a jury might side with the pirates.
- **He provided incentives** to catch pirates: he offered a prize for Teach's capture.

However, Spotswood is best known for his direct actions against Teach. In 1718, Spotswood planned an attack on

Teach's known hideouts in North Carolina, which included the town of Bath and the small island of Ocracoke. The plan was put into action on 17 November and the officer in charge, Lieutenant Maynard, caught up with Teach at Ocracoke by 21 November. He and his crew attacked the next day and Teach's head was cut off in the fighting. The combined actions of a governor and the Royal Navy had finally put an end to Teach's career in piracy.

Key term

Board of Trade*

Government advisers who looked after the colonies of the British Empire. It checked any new colonial laws and helped to appoint new governors.

End of the golden age

In the attempt to capture pirates, more were killed than ended up on trial. As a result, the number of active pirates dropped rapidly. By 1725, only 200 were left in American waters. A year later, very few remained. The golden age of piracy was over.

Summary

- A mixture of immigrants came to British America. This helped to improve the economy, but also created tensions between groups in colonial society.
- Trade with Britain and the West Indies helped the economy to grow.
- Tobacco was a very important product in some of the southern colonies. Demand for it in Britain went up.
- Tea became popular with colonists. This shared habit helped to strengthen the bond with Britain.
- Piracy severely damaged trade in American waters between 1715 and 1725.
- The British government, including King George I and parliament, took steps to end piracy.

Checkpoint

Strengthen

S1 Who were the main immigrant groups that arrived after 1713?

S2 Describe, in detail, three reasons why the economy of British America grew.

S3 Choose one pirate. What actions did he take that damaged trade?

Challenge

C1 Explain how each of the following affected the colonies' relationship with Britain:

    a the way the colonies were governed   **b** increased demand for tobacco in Britain

    c the presence of pirates in American waters.

C2 What other features of colonial society could have affected the colonies' relationship with Britain?

How confident do you feel about your answers to these questions? If you're not sure you answered them well, try to find a piece of specific evidence to back up each of the points in the summary box.

1.2 Slavery in North America

Learning outcomes

- Understand the key features of the slave trade and the significance of the British monopoly on the supply of slaves to the Spanish colonies.
- Understand the impact of slavery on the development of tobacco and rice plantations.
- Understand the position of slaves within colonial society, their treatment, and the significance of the Spanish decision to offer runaways their freedom.

The slave trade and the 'Atlantic triangle'

British America relied upon enslaved Africans for its success in the 1700s. Between 1701 and 1720, the colonists bought 30,000 slaves. This figure more than doubled in the next 20 years, when 70,000 more slaves were transported to North America. Many of these men and women ended up in the colonies as a result of a trading system called the 'Atlantic triangle' (see Figure 1.6).

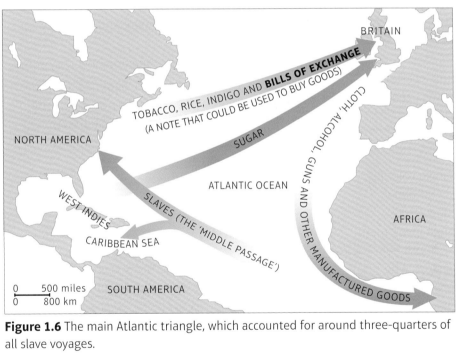

Figure 1.6 The main Atlantic triangle, which accounted for around three-quarters of all slave voyages.

Extend your knowledge

The middle passage

The journey from West Africa to America, known as the middle passage, usually took six weeks. The conditions were awful, as slaves were kept manacled in tightly packed groups below deck. They lived in a state of constant fear because the crew often beat and abused them to prevent rebellion. As a result of this mistreatment, poor hygiene and disease, around 18% of slaves died on the journey.

Most of the slaves who were transported to North America as part of the Atlantic triangle were sold in the southern colonies of Virginia, Maryland and the Carolinas. For example, between 1721 and 1740, 64,000 out of the 70,000 newly arrived slaves went to work in the southern colonies. It was here that they had the most significant impact, as they:

- **provided a cheap workforce**: the tobacco and rice industries needed lots of workers
- **had a variety of skills**: many Africans had experience working with the crops the colonists grew
- **made up a large part of the local population**: in South Carolina, the majority of the population was enslaved.

British monopoly on supplying slaves to Spanish colonies

In 1713, Britain was given the right of *asiento* by the Spanish king. This right gave Britain a monopoly* on the supply of slaves to the Spanish colonies, which included much of South America and the island of Cuba. The terms of the *asiento* were:

- Britain paid a fee of £7.5 million to buy the *asiento*.
- The British had to carry 4,800 slaves each year for 30 years to the Spanish colonies.
- A regular payment would be made to the Spanish king for each slave traded.

The *asiento* continued until 1739, when a war with Spain, called the War of Jenkins' Ear, ended the agreement before the 30-year term had finished.

Key term

Monopoly*

An exclusive right to trade or manufacture a certain product. In the early 1700s, a monopoly was usually given to a company.

The significance of the asiento

The monopoly to supply slaves to the Spanish colonies was given to the newly formed South Sea Company. During the *asiento* period, it shipped around 75,000 slaves to Spanish America, which led to huge investment in the British slave trade. For example, the South Sea Company received £9 million from its investors, who bought shares* in the company. Some grew very rich after selling the shares when their value had risen.

Key term

Shares*

The purchase of part of the ownership of a company.

However, the company did not perform as well as its investors hoped. It suffered from two major problems in its trade with Spain.

- Smugglers sold slaves to Spanish America without permission from the South Sea Company. This extra competition meant the price the company could charge per slave was reduced.

- War interrupted trade to the Spanish colonies. For example, a war with Spain between 1718 and 1720 temporarily stopped the trade.

These problems reduced profits and the share price dropped. In 1720, the amount a share was worth fell from £1,000 in June to £180 in September. Many investors lost huge amounts of money. The *asiento*, which continued until 1739, had failed to create the fabulous profits the British had hoped for.

Activities ?

1 Look at Source A below. Identify two points from the source that prove the slave trade was important in Carolina.

2 Draw an outline copy of Figure 1.6. Add labels that state:
   a who benefits at each stage and how they benefit
   b who suffers at each stage and how they suffer.

3 Create a spider diagram with 'Significance of the slave trade and *asiento* in the centre. Then add branches related to how they might affect:
   a colonial society
   b economic developments
   c the emergence of piracy.

Source A

A description of the slave trade in Charleston, South Carolina by a slave trader called Henry Laurens. It is from 1755 and recalls a sale of slaves that went badly.

We had as many purchasers as we could have wished for had we three times the number [of slaves] for sale but... many of them became extremely angry that we should invite them down from eighty or ninety miles distance to look at a parcel of 'refuse slaves', as they called them and, with some difficulty, [we] prevailed on them to wait [for] the sale... We were willing to believe that Captain [Caleb] Godfrey obtained the best [slaves] he could but, really, they were a wretched cargo, such a one we would not have touched could we have been excused from it... [The slaves] seemed past all hopes of recovery... they are a most scabby flock... Several have extreme[ly] sore eyes, three very puny children and, add to this, the worst infirmity of all others with which six or eight are attended... [is] old age.

The impact of slavery on the development of tobacco plantations

Source B

An 18th-century image of slaves working on an tobacco plantation in Virginia c1750. The engraving also shows a tobacco plant, to a different scale.

Slavery was very important to the development of tobacco plantations in the Chesapeake regions of Virginia, Maryland and North Carolina. The crop required a lot of labourers, as one person was needed for every two acres of tobacco. This person would have to work hard at repetitive tasks, six days a week, from sunrise to sunset. Slavery provided a source of workers who could be forced to work under these conditions.

Slaves influenced the growth of tobacco plantations in a number of ways. They:

- **provided the labour force** for plantations to grow: over 55,000 Africans were enslaved and taken to Chesapeake between 1700 and 1740
- **helped create an efficient production system:** slaves were split into gangs of around 12, which could be supervised by one trusted slave foreman, with a single white overseer to check up on many slave gangs
- **could offer advice on how to improve farming techniques:** tobacco was a crop that was grown in parts of West Africa, so some slaves had experience of its production.

The consequences of slavery for tobacco plantations

The effect of a cheap labour force, which could be made to work hard through brutal treatment, was that the production of tobacco rose dramatically. In 1700, 28 million pounds of tobacco (in weight) was produced in North America. By 1760, that figure had risen to 80 million pounds.

Profits

Despite the massive increase in supply, the demand for tobacco and the use of slaves helped to keep tobacco growing profitable. For example, in one Maryland county in the 1730s, a landowner with slaves had on average £479 more in total wealth (equivalent to around £65,000 today) than a tobacco grower without slaves.

Society

This economic development came at a cost. From 1720 onwards, there were more slaves who worked on tobacco plantations than indentured servants. The economy of the Chesapeake was now entirely dependent on the enslaved workforce, which made up about 35% of the total population.

The impact of slavery on the development of rice plantations

Figure 1.7 This 19th-century illustration shows a typical rice plantation in South Carolina. It shows black slaves working on the crop.

The slaves provided a similar workforce on the rice plantations of South Carolina to that on the tobacco plantations. However, this was not the only reason that slavery played a significant role in large-scale rice production. Figure 1.8 demonstrates that, without slaves, it is unlikely that the rice crop would ever have been introduced, or a workforce found to grow it.

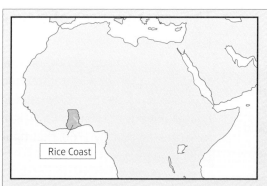

Slaves provided knowledge: some came from the Rice Coast of West Africa and helped to teach planters how to grow the crop.

Slaves did hard work: they performed the tough tasks, like ditch-digging, that rice required.

Slaves worked in harsh conditions: forced labour meant that white planters could grow rice in the disease-ridden swamps of South Carolina, without having to live alongside it themselves.

Slaves took on responsibilities: because white planters lived in towns, slaves were given more responsibility for the rice crop and given tasks that could be checked on less frequently.

Figure 1.8 The impact of slavery on rice plantations.

Source C

A letter from a doctor to a friend in England, written around 1750. It describes the work of rice slaves.

Our Staple [main] Commodity for some years has been Rice, and Tilling, planting, Hoeing, Reaping, Threshing [and] Pounding have all been done merely by the poor Slaves here. Labour and the Loss of many of their Lives testified [to] the Fatigue they Underwent, in [satisfying the greed]... of their Masters. You may easily guess what a Tedious, Laborious, and slow Method it is of Cultivating Lands to Till it all by Hand, and then to plant 100, 120 Acres of Land by Hand, but the worst comes last for after the Rice is threshed, they beat it all in the hand in large Wooden Mortars [bowls] to clean it from the Husk, which is a very hard and severe operation as each Slave is tasked at Seven Mortars for One Day, and each Mortar Contains three pecks [about 26 litres] of Rice.

The consequences of slavery for rice plantations

The hardworking slaves of South Carolina helped rice plantation owners make a lot of profit. They earned around four times more than tobacco planters, and their crops became more and more popular. In 1700, around 400,000 pounds (in weight) of rice were sold abroad. By 1740, this had risen to 43 million pounds. Slaves had become so much a part of South Carolina's economic success that, by 1720, they outnumbered the free population.

Activities ?

1 Write a speech to explain the use of slaves, from one of the following points of view:

   a an 18th-century tobacco planter

   b an 18th-century rice planter.

2 Read out your speech to a partner and get them to try to memorise some of your key arguments. Test them to see how many arguments they can remember.

3 Discuss with your partner how a slave would feel about these arguments. Try to think of three reasons why a tobacco or rice slave might be angry about them.

The impact of slavery on colonial society

Slavery had a greater impact on the southern colonies than it did elsewhere in British America. Slaves were central to the economy, which affected the type of society that developed. These effects were:

- **A huge gap between rich and poor**: slave owners made big profits, which pushed up the price of land. This made it difficult for poor labourers to buy land and compete with the rich.

- **A lack of opportunity for poor labourers**: slave labour was cheaper in the long term than free labour*, which made it difficult for servants and labourers to get a job.

- **Fewer free white colonists than slaves**: slaves provided the main workforce, so they outnumbered the free white population.

The situation was different in the mixed economies* of New England and the middle colonies. The colonists here also had slaves, but these were fewer in number and were not the main source of labour (see Figure 1.9). Their influence on the society that developed in the north was therefore much smaller.

Key terms

Free labour*

Workers who perform a job in return for wages or goods. In British America, this refers to workers who were not slaves or indentured servants.

Mixed economies*

When a range of different goods and services are produced or provided. This differs from the reliance on a single crop found in the southern colonies.

The position of slaves within society

Figure 1.9, on the next page, shows how the role of slaves differed throughout British America but, despite these differences, their position in society remained the same. Slaves were at the lowest level in colonial society and were seen as property, which meant they had no legal rights. For example, a slave could not give evidence in court.

New England colonies	Middle colonies	Southern colonies

Most slaves lived in urban areas, working as sailors and dockworkers, or lived and worked alongside white labourers on small farms. They made up around 3% of the population.	Slaves in the middle colonies were in a similar position to those in New England, but they made up more of the population (6%). They did similar jobs to poor white people, such as assistants to craftsmen, domestic servants or farm labourers.	Most slaves lived in the countryside and worked on huge tobacco or rice plantations. Unlike the other colonies, slaves worked in far greater numbers in the south and made up between 33% and 67% of the population.

Figure 1.9 Slavery in British America.

Slaves also had little personal freedom. Laws introduced in the 1700s meant a slave could not:

- travel without permission
- sell goods for a profit
- own animals
- gather in large groups
- stay out at night.

These laws were strengthened by the position of a slave's master. It was made legal for a master to treat their slaves however they liked. The result was that slaves had little protection from being brutally treated, raped or beaten to death by their master.

Basic freedoms
Slaves had no legal rights in British America, but they were usually allowed some basic freedoms. These included:

- **free time**: most slaves in South Carolina did not live with their masters. Once they had finished their task for the day, they were free to use their time as they liked, within the set laws
- **freedom of religion**: before 1750, slaves were usually allowed to practise religions brought with them from Africa, or could choose to convert to Christianity.

Skilled slaves
A few slaves managed to escape the hardships of work in the fields. For example, some urban slaves developed skills such as cabinet making or ironworking. Other slaves, usually women, became domestic slaves and worked in a planter's house. Both of these types of slaves were generally treated better, but were also at constant risk from their owner's anger or sexual demands.

Impact on colonial society
The information above demonstrates how slaves were pushed to the bottom of colonial society. However, this had a couple of unwanted effects for the society of the southern colonies.

- **It created fear**: the huge number of black slaves, with few rights and little hope of advancement, made white colonists live in fear of rebellion.
- **It created dependence**: slaves worked on the colonists' plantations, learned skilled jobs in the urban areas and served them in their homes. The upper ranks of colonial society relied upon slavery.

24

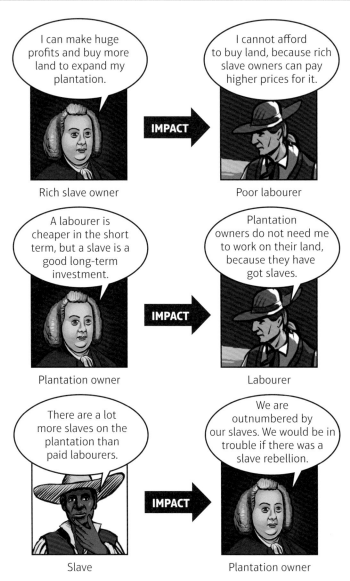

Figure 1.10 The impact of slavery on colonial society in the southern colonies.

The treatment of fugitive slaves

Many slaves found their position in colonial society unbearable and tried to run away. Some rebelled and attacked their masters. These actions were treated as crimes and punished severely. A runaway could be whipped, chained up or branded. A rebellious slave was dealt with even more harshly. In 1714, a law was passed in South Carolina that introduced the death penalty for an attack on a white person by a slave.

Impact on colonial society

In order to capture, return and punish fugitive* slaves, militia* groups were formed. These were usually made up of poor white men who would hunt for the black slaves. The effect was to increase the divisions in colonial society between white and black people.

The significance of Spain's decision to protect runaway slaves in Florida

In 1733, the king of Spain restated an offer the previous king had made in 1693, which was designed to weaken South Carolina's economy. He promised freedom to any slave who escaped the British colonies and made it to Florida. In return, they had to convert to Catholicism* and serve an indenture period of four years. This was an attractive offer, which got even better in 1738, when the requirement to serve an indenture was removed. Fugitive slaves now had a place they could escape to and live their lives in relative safety.

> ### Key terms
>
> **Fugitive***
>
> A person who has escaped their imprisonment. On a slave plantation, a runaway was considered a fugitive.
>
> **Militia***
>
> An armed group of ordinary people who are not usually soldiers, but can fight when needed.
>
> **Catholicism***
>
> A form of Christianity led by the pope in Rome. Spain was a Catholic country in the 18th century, whereas England was Protestant.

The results

In response to the king's offer, a small number of British America's slaves ran away to St Augustine in Spanish Florida. By 1738, the number of runaways had risen to around 100 and the former slaves had established their own town, called Mose. They felt safe because it was now impossible for their former owners to legally reclaim them. For example, Captain Caleb Davis tried to take his slaves back in December 1738, but the governor of Florida stopped him. The residents of Mose also took active steps to ensure their own freedom. They formed a militia and tried to prevent any British expansion in their direction.

Figure 1.11 The options available to a slave in South Carolina in 1738.

Impact on colonial society

Although 100 runaway slaves could not seriously threaten British America, they could unsettle colonial society. The offer of freedom and the presence of former slaves in Florida had a number of consequences.

- **It encouraged rebellion**: slaves knew they had a place to flee to, which led to rebellion. The Stono Rebellion of 1739 is an example of this (see page 27).
- **A new law was passed**: in 1740, South Carolina's government passed a new slave code (see page 28), which was also influenced by the Stono Rebellion.
- **It led to military action**: The Mose militia destroyed a British fort in 1739. In response, James Oglethorpe attacked Mose in 1740, but failed to destroy the town permanently.

Activity ?

Create your own copy of Figure 1.11, but replace the slave with a white colonist from South Carolina. Fill in what he might think about the existence of Mose.

Summary

- Huge numbers of slaves arrived via the Atlantic triangle. Most ended up in the southern colonies.
- The *asiento* gave Britain a monopoly on the supply of slaves to the Spanish colonies.
- Slavery helped tobacco and rice plantations to grow rapidly.
- Slaves were treated poorly and held the lowest position in colonial society.
- Colonists depended on slaves for their income, but were afraid that they might rebel.
- Spain's decision to protect runaway slaves increased the risk of slave rebellion.

Checkpoint

Strengthen

S1 What were the key features of the Atlantic triangle?

S2 Describe, in detail, two effects that slavery had on the tobacco and rice plantations.

S3 What evidence can you find that slaves were treated badly in British America?

Challenge

C1 Below are three different ways to measure the significance of slavery to the situation in British America. Use the detail in this part of the chapter to help you explain your answers to the following questions.

- **a** Did slavery affect a lot of people?
- **b** Did slavery change people's attitudes?
- **c** Did slavery influence events at the time?

C2 How else could you measure the significance of slavery to British America?

How confident do you feel about your answers to these questions? If you're not sure you answered them well, find one fact for each part of C1 and add them to your original answer.

1.3 Problems within the colonies

Learning outcomes

- Understand the key features of the Stono Rebellion (1739) and its consequences.
- Understand the main events of the New York Conspiracy (1741) and its consequences.
- Understand the attempts to collect customs revenue, the problems smuggling caused and the controls placed on the fur trade.

Slave revolts in the Carolinas: the Stono Rebellion, 1739

Background

The only major slave revolt in British America took place in South Carolina in September 1739. The slaves in this colony were in a unique position, which gave them the opportunity to revolt. Firstly, they were in the majority, as 67% of the population were slaves. Secondly, they had a place to run to, as South Carolina was close to Spanish Florida. If they reached it, the slaves could receive their freedom (see page 26). Any revolt in South Carolina therefore stood a chance of success.

However, it was not until 1739 that slaves were pushed into open rebellion. That summer, yellow fever* had struck the colony for the first time in seven years, and many died. By September, when the rice harvest was at its height, the slaves who had survived were struggling to cope. This was the moment they chose to revolt, due to a couple of reasons.

- **A rumour that war with Spain** was coming had spread to South Carolina in early September, which meant the colonists would be distracted from chasing rebels.
- **A Security Act** was to become active on 29 September. If the slaves were going rebel, they had a better chance of success before it came into force (see also Extend your knowledge on page 28).

Key term

Yellow fever*

A tropical disease spread by mosquitos which causes internal bleeding, a high fever, vomiting and yellowing of the skin. Many sufferers die after a week, but some survive with good care.

Events

On Sunday 9 September 1739, about 20 slaves met at Hutchenson's Store near the Stono River Bridge. They stole guns and ammunition from the store, beheaded the owners and made for Florida. On their journey, they killed 20 white people and burned seven plantations. They also beat drums, which attracted around 100 slaves to join them. By the afternoon, they felt confident enough to take a break near the Edisto River. Here they waited for more slaves to join their rebellion.

In the meantime, the lieutenant governor of South Carolina had spotted the rebels, at 11 a.m. He took prompt action and gathered the local militia. By 4 p.m., the well-armed militia was ready to strike the rebels. It burst onto the field near the Edisto River and killed many of the slaves, but around 30 escaped. The militia caught up with most of them a week later, but a few still remained on the run and were gradually hunted down. The last was caught in 1742.

Consequences

The consequences for the rebels were severe. Those who were killed in battle had their heads stuck on mileposts* throughout the colony. The rest, who were eventually hunted down, were executed in a variety of brutal ways. For example, some were hung in chains and left to be eaten by birds and other wild animals. These extreme punishments, designed to make an example of the rebels, indicate the high level of fear created by the rebellion.

Key term

Mileposts*

Road signs indicating the distance to places.

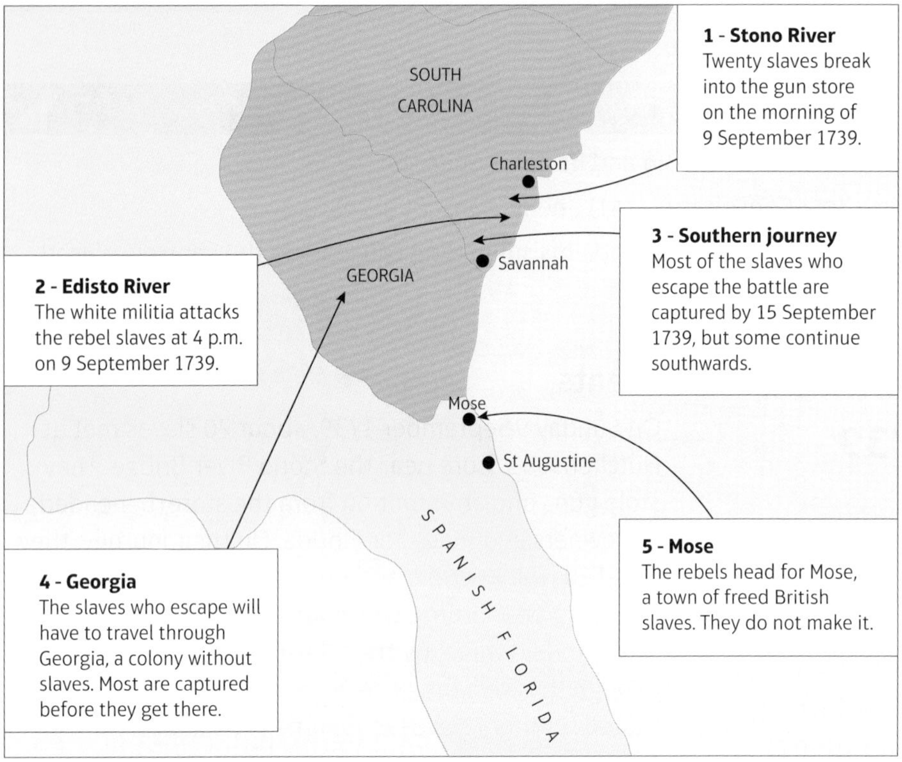

1 – Stono River
Twenty slaves break into the gun store on the morning of 9 September 1739.

SOUTH CAROLINA

Charleston

3 – Southern journey
Most of the slaves who escape the battle are captured by 15 September 1739, but some continue southwards.

Savannah

GEORGIA

2 – Edisto River
The white militia attacks the rebel slaves at 4 p.m. on 9 September 1739.

Mose

St Augustine

SPANISH FLORIDA

5 – Mose
The rebels head for Mose, a town of freed British slaves. They do not make it.

4 – Georgia
The slaves who escape will have to travel through Georgia, a colony without slaves. Most are captured before they get there.

Figure 1.12 The key stages of the Stono Rebellion, 1739.

Extend your knowledge

The Security Act, 1739
South Carolina's slaves were usually given free time on a Sunday to complete their own chores and socialise. This made it the most likely day for a rebellion. In response to this risk, the Security Act made it compulsory for white men to carry a gun on Sundays.

Key consequence: fear of future revolt

Fear of another rebellion led the colonists to take action. They wanted to prevent future revolts and turned to their government for help. The South Carolina government introduced a new slave code, which included several measures.

- **Greater restrictions on slave freedom:** the Negro Act, introduced in 1740, fined planters who could not control their slaves, removed the right to grant slaves their freedom and restricted the movements of slaves.

- **Limitations on slave numbers:** a high tax was added to the purchase of slaves from abroad and the money was used to encourage European immigration. This stabilised the ratio between black and white colonists for about ten years.

- **Reducing the causes of rebellion:** a fine was introduced for masters who dealt with their slaves too harshly. This was an attempt to improve the way slaves were treated.

Interpretation 1

An extract from Kenneth Morgan's book *Slavery and the British Empire*, published in 2007. It explores the significance of the Stono Rebellion.

The collapse of the Stono revolt was not surprising: there was no unanimity among the blacks involved about its purpose and the afternoon pause near the Edisto River gave the white forces time to organize and counter-attack. But though it seems an exaggeration to view such a short outbreak of black violence as a defining moment in the history of South Carolina and of race relations in North America, it left long-lasting fears among the white minority… about the potential for similar revolts in the future.

Activities ?

1 Create a storyboard of the events of the Stono Rebellion, but leave one space blank at the start. Make sure you include causes, events and consequences in your storyboard.

2 Look back at pages 22 and 25 about rice plantations and the Spanish offer of freedom. Choose one piece of information to fill in the blank on your storyboard.

3 Kenneth Morgan has written an interpretation of the Stono Rebellion (Interpretation 1). Find evidence from this part of the chapter for his claims that: 'the collapse of the Stono revolt was not surprising', it was 'a defining moment in the history of South Carolina' and that 'it left long-lasting fears'.

Exam-style question, Section A

Write a narrative account analysing the key events in the years 1739–40 leading to the suppression of slave rights in South Carolina.

You may use the following in your answer:

• the Stono Rebellion, 1739

• the Negro Act, 1740.

You **must** also use information of your own.   **8 marks**

Exam tip

This question targets your ability to write an analytical narrative. It is important to include the events of the Stono Rebellion, and their consequences, in your answer.

The New York Conspiracy, 1741
Background

In early 1741, the leaders of New York convinced themselves that there was a slave and Catholic plot to burn the city. They were anxious because recent events had made the risk of a rebellion a real possibility.

• **The Stono Rebellion**: around 20% of New York's population was enslaved. It was feared that the rebellion in South Carolina would inspire others in British America.

• **The War of Jenkins' Ear**: a war with Catholic Spain had broken out in British America in 1739. New York was a port city, which made it a possible target for a Spanish attack.

• **A tough winter**: the winter had been long and severe. There had been riots over food prices. It was possible the poor white population might join up with slaves to rebel.

The New York Conspiracy trials

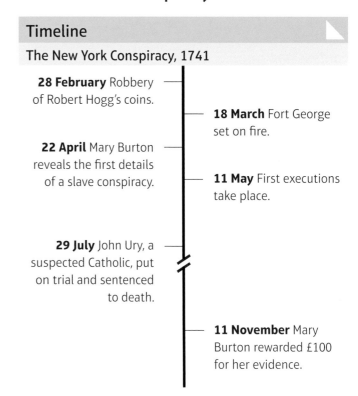

Timeline
The New York Conspiracy, 1741

28 February Robbery of Robert Hogg's coins.

18 March Fort George set on fire.

22 April Mary Burton reveals the first details of a slave conspiracy.

11 May First executions take place.

29 July John Ury, a suspected Catholic, put on trial and sentenced to death.

11 November Mary Burton rewarded £100 for her evidence.

Burglary
On 28 February 1741, a few precious coins were stolen from the home of a merchant called Robert Hogg. As a result, three slaves accused of theft, and a white family accused of handling stolen goods, were put on trial. The earliest evidence that emerged at their trial hinted that the theft was part of a wider conspiracy.

Fires
Suspicion of conspiracy grew worse on 18 March 1741 when Fort George, home to the governor, was set alight. Fires like this worried the people of New York because they lived in a city of tightly packed wooden houses. In this environment, one house fire could quickly become a general inferno. Another 13 fires that followed therefore created fear and fed rumours.

29

The conspiracy

The most popular rumour in March 1741 was that the fires were part of a co-ordinated plot to destroy the city. It was an idea that the leaders of New York began to accept in April. They were convinced by evidence from a white servant called Mary Burton, who told a court that she had overheard the plotters. She claimed that they had met in the tavern where she worked, planned the fire at Fort George and obtained guns. It was her evidence that turned a robbery investigation into an investigation of a general conspiracy.

Confessions

After Burton's testimony*, events spiralled out of control. Many slaves, white Catholics, black Spanish sailors and poor white people were arrested and put on trial. These men and women were very keen to confess and accuse others because the governor had offered both a pardon and reward if they did so. Their confessions named other people as conspirators, who were arrested and then gave even more names. The result was that, by early August, around 150 people had been put on trial.

Key term

Testimony*

Evidence given in court. Most of the individuals accused as part of the New York Conspiracy were named in testimony presented to the court.

Extend your knowledge

The trial of John Ury

In New York, simply being a Catholic priest was a criminal offence. A man named John Ury was accused of this crime and also charged with an attempt to gather Catholics, in a variety of disguises, to join the conspiracy. His trial, on 29 July 1741, was short: the jury found him guilty. His execution showed that the authorities feared that both slaves and Catholics were involved in the conspiracy.

Why do you think the leaders of New York were afraid of the Catholics in their city?

Source A

The evidence of Mary Burton. She presented this to the court on 22 April 1741. It is the first description of a conspiracy to burn down the city.

2. 'That Caesar, Prince and Mr Philipse's negro man (Cuffee) used to meet frequently at her master's house, and that she had heard them (the negroes) talk frequently of burning the fort; and that they would go down to the fly and burn the whole town; and that her master and mistress said, they would aid and assist them as much as they could…

4. 'That Cuffee used to say, that a great many people had too much, and others too little…

7. 'That she has known at times, seven or eight guns in her master's house, and some swords, and that she has seen twenty or thirty negroes at one time in her master's house; and that at such large meetings, the three aforesaid negroes, Cuffee, Prince, and Caesar, were generally present, and most active…'

Activity

Plan a role play about how the judges might react to Mary Burton's evidence (Source A). Consider:

  a Do they believe her? Why?

  b How should they react to this information?

Consequences

By the time the trials came to an end, 31 slaves and four whites had been executed. A further 72 slaves had been deported for their part in the conspiracy. This suggests that the leaders of New York believed a rebellion could have happened in 1741. It led them to take action to limit the freedom of movement of all black people in the colony. These actions included:

- a law against fetching water from wells other than the nearest one
- a restriction on horseback riding, meaning that black people were no longer allowed to ride on a Sunday, because it was thought they might use their day off to meet up and plan a rebellion.

It was hoped that these laws would remove the opportunity for slaves and free black people to meet and conspire together. This must have calmed the nerves of New York's leadership because when suspicious fires began again in March 1742, the conspiracy trials did not restart.

Source B

A map called *A Plan of the City and Environs of New York as they were in 1742–44*. It was drawn from memory in 1813 and shows two gallows, where conspirators were hanged, and bodies being burned.

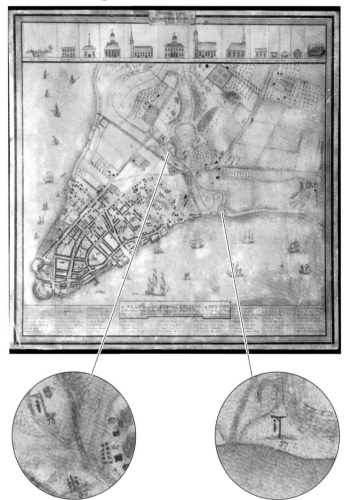

Attempts to collect customs revenue

The British government wanted to profit from its empire. One way to do this was to raise money through the collection of customs duties*. By 1713, a number of controls had been put in place. Each North American colony had a customs officer*, who collected the duties, authorised the loading and unloading of ships and checked their paperwork. Customs officers also had powers to make sure controls were effective, such as:

- the right to arrest those who broke the rules and put them on trial in an admiralty court: this type of court did not have a jury and the governor chose the judge
- the power to use writs of assistance*, which allowed the customs officer to search for illegally imported goods.

Key terms

Customs duties*

Taxes collected on trade goods. These were charged on goods brought into the colony (imports) and on certain named goods that were shipped abroad for sale (exports).

Customs officer*

The person in charge of a colony's customs service.

Writs of assistance*

An early form of search warrant, needed to search a private property legally.

Location	Job	Main role
Harbour	Tideswaiter	Went on board a ship as it sailed into the harbour.
Harbour	Landwaiter	In control of the quay and checked no goods left the ship without permission.
Harbour	Surveyor and searcher	Inspected ships and oversaw the jobs at the harbour.
Coastline	Riding surveyor	Rode up and down the coast on horseback to search for smugglers.
Customs house	Comptroller	Checked the records of the customs officer.
Customs house	Naval officer	Kept records of the ships that entered and left the port.
Colonial government	Surveyor-general	Inspected the entire system of customs collection.

There was a complex system in place to help customs officers and to check up on them. The table above lists some of the jobs that made up this system.

Activity ?

Choose three jobs from the table. Explain how each could improve the collection of customs revenue.

Increasing customs revenue

During the period 1713–41, parliament also used legislation to increase customs revenue* in British America. In 1733, the Molasses Act placed a very high duty on imported molasses from foreign colonies. It meant that it was cheaper to buy molasses from the British West Indies. As a result, the duty collected on imports from the British West Indies rose from £8,000 in 1730 to £40,000 immediately after the Act.

Key term

Customs revenue*

The amount collected from the tax on trade goods. In British America, the revenue collected from customs was sent to Britain.

The problems with customs collection

The revenue collected by the customs service was limited by a number of problems.

- **Absent officials**: the jobs in the service were often given to important men in England who wanted the salary, but not the job. Instead, they sent poorly paid deputies who accepted bribes to improve their income.

- **Overwork**: the job of a customs officer was too big for one person. They had to check trading laws were followed, ensure the coast was guarded, deal with lawbreakers and collect duties.

- **Difficulties of control**: most officers sympathised with the traders rather than the distant British parliament. If they did not agree with a law, they did little to enforce it.

The result of these problems was that new measures were ignored after the initial funding to enforce them ended. For example, £330 was collected under the terms of the Molasses Act in 1733–34, but this dropped to £69 in 1737–38. The problems also improved the chances of success for a smuggler*.

Key term

Smuggler*

A trader who illegally avoids the payment of customs duties on their cargo, or imports and exports goods forbidden by trade laws.

The problem of smuggling

The actions of smugglers threatened the level of customs revenue that could be collected. Usually, the goods that were smuggled into British America were the ones that had the highest duty or were carefully controlled by British trade laws. The most common products were molasses from the Spanish or French West Indies and tea from the East Indies.

Smugglers used a number of methods to avoid the payment of duties on these goods. They:

- landed their ships on a quiet section of the coastline, unloaded their cargo and then carried on to the official port with an empty hold
- carried false paperwork, which was difficult to check because of the time it took to communicate with Britain
- kept their cargo in a ship's store then secretly unloaded it from there: a ship was permitted to keep items in a small store, for the crew's own use, without payment of duties
- bribed the customs officer to report their ship's cargo as carrying fewer goods than they really were, in order to pay a lower rate of duty.

Impact of smuggling

It is very difficult to judge the impact of smuggling due to the lack of official records. There is some evidence that it affected the collection of the duty set out in the Molasses Act (1733) because the revenue collected from the British West Indies fell rapidly in the late 1730s. This suggests that the colonists continued to buy foreign molasses and avoided the duty in British America through smuggling.

However, the smuggling did not stop a dramatic rise in recorded exports from Britain to the North American colonies. In 1730–31, £559,000 worth of goods was exported to British America, which rose to £1,179,000 in 1750–51. These official exports, which followed customs rules, would have had customs duties paid on them. Whatever effect smuggling had on the colonies, it had not stopped a huge rise in law-abiding trade.

Attempts to control the fur trade

Another problem the colonists faced was that the British tried to limit the colonial fur trade. Parliament created two measures to do this.

- In 1721, it added fur and skins to the list of goods that had to be sent directly to Britain. They could then be sent on to Europe if required.
- The Hat Act of 1732 was introduced. This stopped the export of beaver-fur hats from each colony. It also added new rules to limit production of the hats.

The 1721 measure had a limited effect because the trade was not a large one. New York was the main colony involved in the fur trade, but did not suffer any serious consequences. Demand in England provided a market for all the fur the colonists could acquire. The only difference was that, instead of shipping its fur to Holland, New York sent 55% more fur to England.

Interpretation 2

An extract from Richard Middleton and Anne Lombard's book *Colonial America: A History to 1763*, published in 2011. It explores the significance of smuggling in British America.

People certainly talked as though smuggling was common, though the evidence suggests that outside the West Indies most merchants obeyed the rules, especially when trading with Europe, since North American vessels were very conspicuous and could be easily policed by their British counterparts… Religion was one reason for such a law-abiding attitude, since conscience clearly dictated that it was improper to deny the king his due… If there were infractions, these are likely to have occurred as a result of the 1733 Molasses Act, which seemed to have been passed to allow British sugar planters to live in idleness and luxury.

Activities ?

1 Imagine you are in New England in 1733. In pairs, each person should do one of these tasks:

   a Prepare to interview a new customs officer. Write down five questions to ask them.

   b Prepare to be interviewed for a position as customs officer. Make a few notes to take to your interview.

2 Conduct your mock interview. Award your partner a point every time they make a specific reference to 1730s British America.

3 Write a letter to the candidate or interviewer.

   a If you are the interviewer, will you offer them the job? Explain why.

   b If you are the candidate, do you plan to accept the job? Explain why.

The hat trade in New England and New York also continued to do well because more colonists chose to buy locally produced hats. As a result, the import of hats from England fell by £1,000 between 1730 and 1735. Any hats that could not be sold in the colonies were shipped off to the West Indies because the Acts were not strictly enforced and trade continued.

Extend your knowledge

Problems in the fur trade

Beaver pelts (furs) were in huge demand in England and most of the supply came from trade with Native Americans by British colonists. However, by the 1700s, beaver numbers had begun to fall. This led to competition with the French over an increasingly scarce resource. The British offered to pay higher prices and secured the trade, but beaver numbers continued to drop.

Source C

An engraving of the skilled process of beaver-fur hat production in 1750.

Summary

- The Stono Rebellion (1739) was the biggest slave revolt in British America.
- The rebellion led to the introduction of the Negro Act (1740), which restricted slave freedom.
- The leaders of New York thought there was a slave and Catholic conspiracy to destroy their city in 1741.
- The New York Conspiracy (1741) resulted in limitations on freedom for all black people in New York.
- There were a number of measures to collect customs revenue, but these were not very effective.
- Smuggling and lack of enforcement made it difficult to collect revenue and control trade.

Checkpoint

Strengthen

S1 Re-read the information on the Stono Rebellion. Identify one cause, one event and one consequence.

S2 What were the main events in the early stages of the New York Conspiracy (February to April 1741)?

S3 Give three detailed examples of the problems the British authorities faced in collecting customs revenue.

Challenge

C1 An analytical narrative finds the connections between events. Explain a connection between:

    a the outbreak of war with Spain (1739) and the Stono Rebellion

    b the Stono Rebellion and the New York Conspiracy

    c attempts to collect customs revenue and the problem of smuggling.

C2 Try to make another connection between two events, but this time choose one from this part of the chapter and one from an earlier part of the chapter.

How confident do you feel about your answers to these questions? If you're not sure you answered them well, construct a flow diagram of the key stages in each event or development.

Recap: British settlement in North America, 1713–41

Recall quiz

Have a go at these 10 quick-fire questions:

1 Name three groups that came to the colonies between 1713 and 1741.

2 What percentage of its produce did British America export: 10%, 50% or 90%?

3 Which pirate set up a base in North Carolina?

4 Name one method used to suppress piracy.

5 How many slaves were transported to British America between 1721 and 1740: 10,000, 70,000 or 500,000?

6 In what year was the *asiento* given to the British?

7 In which colony did slaves help on rice plantations?

8 When did the Stono Rebellion begin?

9 List two crimes that slaves were accused of during the New York Conspiracy.

10 Which Act of 1733 was designed to increase customs revenue?

Exam-style question, Section A

Explain **two** of the following:

- The importance of the Piracy Act (1717) for the suppression of piracy
- The importance of the Stono Rebellion (1739) for the government of South Carolina
- The importance of the Molasses Act (1733) for the colonial customs service. **16 marks**

Exam tip

This question targets your ability to explain the importance of an event. Make sure you focus your answer on the difference the event made to the situation or development given in the question.

Activities

1 Copy and complete the table below:

In 1713	In 1741
Most colonists had arrived from…	The new colonists had arrived from…
The most popular drink was…	The most popular drink was…
Piracy was a problem because…	Piracy had been suppressed because…
The British had an exclusive right to trade slaves with…	The *asiento* was over and the British had sent…
The colonies relied on slaves to…	The reliance on slaves had been threatened by…
Slaves could run away to…	Runaway slaves had established their own settlement at…
Britain raised money through…	Britain had struggled to increase customs revenue because…

2 Use the information in this chapter to complete the tasks below.

   a Write a short paragraph explaining how colonial society changed between 1713 and 1741.

   b Create a spider diagram of the main consequences of slavery for British America.

   c Write a paragraph explaining how similar the Stono Rebellion (1739) was to the New York Conspiracy (1741).

Writing historically: building information

When you are asked to write an explanation or analysis, you need to provide as much detailed information as possible.

Learning outcomes

By the end of this lesson, you will understand how to:

- add clear and detailed information to your writing by using relative clauses and noun phrases in apposition.

Definitions

Relative clause: a clause that adds information or modifies a noun, linked with a relative pronoun, e.g. 'who', 'that', 'which', 'where', 'whose'.

Noun phrase in apposition: two noun phrases, positioned side-by-side, the second adding information to the first, e.g. [1] 'South Carolina, [2] a rice-growing colony, relied heavily on slavery'.

How can I add detail to my writing?

Look at a sentence from the response below to this exam-style question:

> Explain the importance of the Stono Rebellion (1739) for the government of South Carolina. **(8 marks)**

Many of the colonists, who were afraid of another rebellion, wanted to limit the increase in the slave population.

The main clause is highlighted in yellow. The relative pronoun is highlighted in green. The relative clause is highlighted in purple.

This noun phrase is modified by this **relative clause**: it provides more information about the colonists.

1. How could you restructure the sentence above using two separate sentences?

2. Why do you think the writer chose to structure these sentences using a main clause and a relative clause instead of writing them as two separate sentences?

Now look at these four sentences taken from the same response:

> *The government introduced the Negro Act in 1740. The Act punished planters if their slaves were given too much freedom. Another law fined masters for treating their slaves too harshly. The government wanted to prevent slaves rebelling again.*

3. How effectively is this information expressed? Write a sentence or two explaining your answer.

4. How could you improve the written expression in the answer above, using relative pronouns?

   a. Rewrite the sentences using relative pronouns to link all the information in **one** sentence.

   b. Now rewrite the sentence using relative pronouns to link the information in **two** sentences.

   c. Which version do you prefer? Is the information most clearly and fluently expressed in one, two or four sentences? Write a sentence or two explaining your choice.

How can I add detail to my writing in different ways?

You can also add detail to a sentence using a **noun phrase in apposition**.

Compare these sentences:

> South Carolina, which was a colony dependent on slavery, treated the rebels harshly.

This uses a relative clause to add information clearly and briefly.

> South Carolina, a colony dependent on slavery, treated the rebels harshly.

This uses a noun phrase in apposition to add the same information even more clearly and briefly.

5. How could you combine the information in the pairs of sentences below using a noun phrase in apposition?

> Escape to Mose was the aim of the rebels. It was a town of freed British slaves.
>
> The government raised money to encourage European immigration to South Carolina. It came from a tax on the purchase of slaves from abroad.

Did you notice?

6. If you remove the relative clause or the noun phrase in apposition from the two sentences at the top of the page, they both still make sense. They are also both separated from the rest of the sentence with commas. Can you explain why? Write a sentence or two explaining your ideas.

Improving an answer

Look at the extract below from another response to the exam question on the previous page:

> The government in South Carolina wanted to reduce the chance that another slave rebellion would succeed. It was afraid of more violence. It tried to limit the increase in the slave population. A high tax was placed on slaves bought from abroad. This decreased the number of newly imported slaves and resulted in an increase in the proportion of migrants coming from Europe. This meant there would be fewer slaves to join a rebellion and more colonists who could stop one.

7. a. Rewrite the information in the answer above, making it as clear and brief as possible. You could use:

- relative clauses
- nouns in apposition.

b. Look carefully at your response to Question 7a. Are all your sentences easy to read and understand, or are some of them too long and confusing? If so, try rewriting them to make their meaning as clear as possible.

02 | A disrupted society, 1742–64

In 1742, the colonists of British America were in a difficult position. Surrounded by the French and Spanish empires, as well as a variety of Native American tribes, they were forever at risk from attack. Even so, they still felt relatively safe. They were colonists of the British Empire and they knew that, if war broke out, their mother country would send troops to defend them.

However, over the next two decades, this relationship began to change. By 1764, the colonists no longer saw themselves as dependent children of an empire. Instead, they believed they were an important part of that empire. This was a belief promoted by a shake-up in colonial society: old religious ideas were being questioned and a new world view spread rapidly. These ideas promoted education, encouraged the colonists to become more united and created celebrities of men like Benjamin Franklin.

However, these ideas alone could not help the colonists feel secure from a foreign threat. One thing that could was a successful war, and two were fought between 1744 and 1763. Thanks to the power of the British Empire, the colonists won both, and this had a huge effect on them. They had fought wars and removed two foreign empires from their borders. The colonies were no longer insecure and heavily dependent on Britain, but instead were confident and ready to grow.

Learning outcomes

By the end of this chapter, you will understand:

- the impact of religious revivals, the Enlightenment and Benjamin Franklin on colonial society
- the significance of King George's War and the French and Indian War for relations between the North American colonists, their neighbours and their mother country
- the effects of the French and Indian War on the North American colonists, the British and the Native Americans.

Learning outcomes

- Understand the impact of the religious revivals on colonial society.
- Understand the effects of the Enlightenment on the religion, politics, education and scientific understanding of the colonists.
- Understand the significance of Benjamin Franklin as a writer, philanthropist and intellectual.

Religious revivals in the middle colonies and New England

In the 1740s, British America experienced a series of religious revivals* that shook up its traditional Protestant* Christian churches. Figure 2.1 illustrates the religious experience of most Christians before this.

The Great Awakening

In the 1720s, a movement called the Great Awakening began. Reaching a high point in the 1740s, it challenged traditional church services with a new, evangelical* style. Instead of a church, huge crowds of up to 20,000 gathered in an open field. A revivalist* preacher stood in the centre and delivered a spontaneous sermon in an enthusiastic, emotional style. The preacher would argue that people were deeply sinful and the only way they could get to heaven was to surrender to God's will there and then. Many in the audience would scream and shout, as they got caught up in the charged atmosphere of the sermon. They hoped to experience a conversion, known as a 'new birth', which provided a deep emotional release and renewed their Christian faith. It was this personal experience that made religion seem more real to the colonists and helped the revivals to spread.

Key terms

Religious revival*

A renewed commitment to a religious faith. Enthusiasm for more traditional forms of Christianity had declined in British America by the 18th century.

Protestant*

A form of Christianity, practised in a number of different ways. Protestantism was the state religion of Britain, and most of the colonists were Protestants.

Evangelical*

A very enthusiastic form of preaching. It was used to encourage people to convert to Christianity, or renew their commitment to it.

Revivalist*

A person who tries to revive or encourage commitment to a belief in God using an evangelical style. Revivalists were also known as 'New Lights', whereas traditionalists are sometimes referred to as 'Old Lights'.

1. Ministers delivered their sermon from a pulpit in a church.

2. The sermon was pre-planned and carefully structured to present a reasoned argument.

3. Ministers were properly educated in colleges.

4. Women were not supposed to speak in church and could not deliver readings.

5. Often, important members of the community had their own seats.

6. Church attendance was stable but not high.

7. The congregation sat and listened.

Figure 2.1 A traditional Christian church service. There were several types of Protestantism in British America, and this diagram shows some of their shared features.

Source A

An 18th-century painting of the revivalist preacher George Whitefield. It was painted by John Collet.

The revivalists: Jonathan Edwards and George Whitefield

Jonathan Edwards was a revivalist minister in Massachusetts who helped to develop the ideas behind the Great Awakening. He wrote a number of books, including *A Faithful Narrative of the Surprising Work of God* in 1737, and in 1739 preached a series of sermons about God's role in history. His most famous sermon, given in 1741, was called – *Sinners in the Hands of an Angry God*, which encouraged people to convert, to avoid an eternity in hell (see Source B). This helped to make the Great Awakening more popular in New England.

In 1739, another revivalist arrived in British America and helped to spread the Great Awakening even further. George Whitefield, a preacher from England, toured the major towns of British America in 1739–41 and 1744–48, giving sermons in the open air (see Source A). These gatherings would attract upwards of 20,000 people and led to huge numbers of conversions. In order to reach an even wider audience, he also published his sermons: 80,000 copies of his publications were printed in America between 1739 and 1745.

Impact of the revivals

Source B

A sermon written by Jonathan Edwards (1703–58), a revivalist preacher from New England. It was delivered in the early 1740s and explores the theme of hell and the need for God's mercy.

The God that holds you over the pit of hell, much as one holds a spider or some loathsome insect over the fire... [hates] you, and is dreadfully provoked. His wrath towards you burns like a fire; he looks upon you as worthy of nothing else but to be cast into the fire.

The energy that preachers poured into their sermons helped to create enthusiasm for religion. For example, in the early 1740s, up to 50,000 people in New England joined churches. Some joined their local church and others became a part of newer Christian groups, like the Methodists or Baptists, who used an evangelical style. The effects spread throughout British America, as preachers toured the colonies from New England to Georgia.

However, their message, which in some ways treated people as equal in the eyes of God, also disrupted the traditions of colonial society.

- **The Great Awakening divided society:** its supporters were from the poorer classes, such as small farmers, and its opponents were colonial leaders and wealthy merchants.

- **It moved power away from the traditional church:** the revivalists put power in the hands of other religious groups, such as the Baptists and Methodists, as well as the members of the congregation.

- **The revivals improved the status of women:** some women were encouraged to preach or to hold prayer meetings. In the past, women had not been allowed to take an active role in church.

- **It led to the conversion of some black people and Native Americans:** the revivalists targeted these groups, and some did convert to Christianity, such as the Narragansett tribe from Rhode Island.

The Great Awakening gave people the confidence to question traditional ideas and figures of authority. For example, when James Davenport went on a preaching tour of New England in 1742 and 1743, he caused a stir in New London. He claimed the local ministers were useless, which called their authority into question. He also encouraged the residents to burn books and therefore challenge old ideas. His actions demonstrate the unsettling effect the Great Awakening could have in some colonies.

Long-term effects

The Great Awakening was not a cause of the American Revolution (see page 79), but it did help to make this change possible because:

- **it emphasised the importance of the individual,** which encouraged people to question traditional authority

- **the revivalists used open-air meetings,** which were later used as a method for discussing political ideas.

However, it was a movement that affected Britain, too, and helped to strengthen the colonists' links with the mother country, rather than weaken them at that time.

Interpretation 1

An extract from the book *The American Pageant* by David Kennedy, Lizabeth Cohen and Thomas Bailey, published in 2002. It explores the significance of the Great Awakening and suggests that it united the American colonists, which is an idea that historians debate.

The Awakening left many lasting effects. Its emphasis on direct, emotive spirituality seriously undermined the older clergy [ministers], whose authority had derived from their education… [It] greatly increased the numbers and the competitiveness of American churches. It encouraged a fresh wave of missionary work among the Indians and even among black slaves, many of whom also attended the mass open-air revivals. It led to the founding of 'new light' centers of higher learning such as Princeton, Brown, Rutgers, and Dartmouth. Perhaps most significant, the Great Awakening was the first spontaneous mass movement of the American people. It tended to break down… boundaries… and contributed to the growing sense that Americans had of themselves as a single people, united by a common history and shared experiences.

Activities ?

1. Draw up a table with two columns headed 'Traditionalist' and 'Revivalist'. Use Figure 2.1 and Source A to help identify the key features of each type of church service.

2. Imagine a revivalist preacher is coming to town. Create a poster from the point of view of either:
   a A small farmer in the 1740s – your poster should attract people to the gathering.
   b A colonial leader in the 1740s – your poster should attract people to their normal church.

3. Swap your poster with another person. Try to identify the following:
   a Who have they targeted their poster at?
   b What arguments have they used to persuade their target audience?
   c Did the poster's designer benefit or suffer as a result of the Great Awakening?

4. Discuss your findings with your partner. Decide what effects a visit from a revivalist preacher might have on a town in British America.

The Enlightenment

The Enlightenment was an intellectual movement that influenced philosophers, scientists and churchmen from the late 17th century onwards. Enlightened thinkers valued reason* and tried to use it as the basis for their arguments. The main features of the Enlightenment in the mid 18th century were:

- **in religion:** a belief that God existed, but did not actively involve himself in running the world. Individuals were in charge of their own lives.
- **in science:** a theory that the world followed a series of natural laws that could be observed. Scientists collected useful information instead of relying on the Bible or other ancient texts.
- **in politics:** a view that the government should protect people's natural rights. If it did not do this, it could be overthrown.

In British America, the Enlightenment persuaded intellectuals to question long-held ideas about the Church, the government and the world they lived in. It encouraged the colonists to tolerate other religions, observe their world more closely and question the way their government worked. It also helped to make a revolution in their government possible because they no longer accepted that their rulers were chosen by God and could not be challenged.

Key term

Reason*

The human ability to think logically about a problem or issue, form an understanding of it and then reach a well thought-through conclusion.

The emphasis on education

Education was one of the core principles of the Enlightenment. As a result, the number of colleges and schools increased. By 1760, six of the colonies had colleges. Princeton (New Jersey) was founded in 1747, King's College (New York) in 1754 and the College of Philadelphia (Pennsylvania) in 1755. In ten years, the number of colleges in British America had doubled.

A similar development occurred in the number of schools available for children of primary and secondary school age. There were several major changes.

- **The growth of schools in the southern colonies:** New England and the middle colonies already had some non-fee-paying schools. This spread to the south and, by 1750, Virginia had ten 'free schools'*.
- **An increase in private schools:** church groups had provided most of the education in New England and the middle colonies. This continued in the 18th century, but the number of fee-paying schools, run by private individuals, also grew rapidly.
- **More schools for small towns in New England:** the 'moving school' system* no longer satisfied some small towns. New Englanders began to club together and set up their own schools for their towns.

Key terms

Free schools*

These were schools that provided a basic education. Only wealthier people had to pay a fee to send their child to one.

'Moving school' system*

A system whereby a school was shared between several towns. The teacher would travel from town to town to teach lessons.

The curriculum

The Enlightenment emphasised the importance of practical knowledge that could be used in day-to-day life. In the 18th century, schools and colleges continued to offer an education in Christianity and the classics*, but also introduced new practical subjects. These included mathematics, accounting, English, history, science, modern languages and navigation. However, these opportunities were only available to boys from families who could afford to pay. The curriculum offered to other groups was more restricted.

Key term

Classics*

The study of classical civilisations, which includes the Roman and ancient Greek empires.

- **Girls from wealthy backgrounds** could receive private tutoring. This focused on areas that were considered part of a woman's world, such as needlework, artistic skills and French.
- **Poorer boys and girls** went to 'free schools', which offered only basic lessons in literacy and numeracy.

The growth of newspapers

Another effect of the Enlightenment was a rapid growth in the number of colonial newspapers. From one newspaper in 1704, the number rose to 22 in 1745 and to 40 in 1776. Most of this growth occurred in towns such as Boston, where there were four newspapers by 1760. It was helped by the expansion of the post office*, which had 65 offices by 1770. These developments meant colonists had created a way to share information across all of British America.

Key term

Post office*

A colony-wide network for delivering post. The first postmaster general was appointed in 1692 to set up a post office system similar to the one in Britain.

The type of information that they chose to share reflected the Enlightenment's emphasis on practical and useful information. It included adverts of goods for sale, lists of runaway slaves and shipping details. It also included other stories to help sell the papers, such as English news of recent inventions, interesting crimes and parliamentary matters. The colonists were therefore kept up to date with developments in their mother country, but could also use the papers to carry out their business dealings.

Interpretation 2

An extract from the book *American Colonies: The Settling of North America* by Alan Taylor, published in 2001. It explores the consequences of the growth in colonial newspapers.

Newspapers both depended upon and contributed to the integration of the British Atlantic… Avoiding local news stories, the colonial press primary copied official items from the London press… The… effect was to draw colonial readers into an English perspective on the world. In 1717 the Boston newspaper publisher declared that the London news was what 'most nearly concerns us'. Sincere rather than ironic, he… [confirmed] the growing dependence of colonial merchants and officials upon a sense of the conditions in Europe.

Pamphlets

Colonial printing presses also produced lots of pamphlets. These were small leaflets, usually under 24 pages long. Most contained religious sermons and vivid descriptions of hell, but there were other forms of popular material. These included biographies of criminals, the tales of travellers to distant lands and reports of new, often fake, medical treatments.

Source C

Adverts for shipping from the *Pennsylvania Gazette*, placed by two captains and aimed at potential passengers or traders who needed to transport goods. It was printed in 1750.

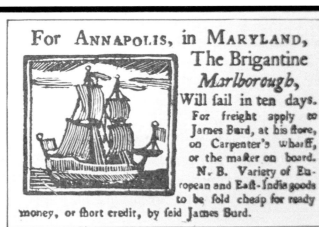

These pamphlets were important because they were relatively cheap and reached a wide audience. They were written to be read aloud, which happened in inns and taverns throughout British America. This helped to create a new way to get information and ideas out to ordinary people, which would be especially important in the lead up to the American Revolution (see 'Thomas Paine' on page 79).

The growth of public libraries

A further consequence of the Enlightenment was the rise of subscription libraries*. These were public in the sense that they made books available to those who could afford a subscription fee. By 1760, there were 20 in British America, providing a wide variety of books. Subscribers could borrow:

- **traditional works:** classical texts and sermons
- **practical books**: legal works and scientific pamphlets
- **fiction:** novels, plays and poems.

The availability of these books, which would have been expensive to buy individually, helped to spread Enlightenment ideas to the middle classes. It also encouraged subscribers to think more deeply about traditional ideas from Christianity and classical civilisations.

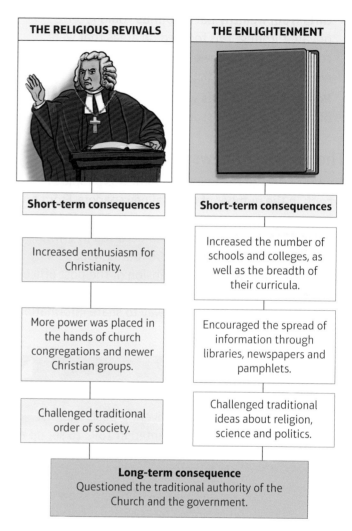

Figure 2.2 The consequences of the religious revivals and the Enlightenment.

Key term

Subscription library*

An organisation that lent books to its members in return for a joining and annual subscription fee. Access to the library collection encouraged people to carry out their own, self-directed, learning.

Activities ?

1 Create a flow chart with 'The Enlightenment' in the first box. In the second layer, add direct consequences of the Enlightenment (e.g. growth of schools).
2 In the third layer, identify how that might affect colonial society (e.g. a more literate population).
3 In the fourth layer, suggest whether this would disrupt colonial society or help bring order to it.

The significance of Benjamin Franklin

Benjamin Franklin (1706–90) was one of the most well-known colonists. He was heavily influenced by Enlightenment ideals and tried to put them into practice. He lived most of his life in Philadelphia, where he worked as a printer until 1748. When he retired from printing, he dedicated the rest of his life to government service. He wrote, conducted scientific experiments, invented things and helped to improve his local community.

A writer

Franklin wrote in a wide variety of formats throughout his life, which included essays, stories and scientific works. He is well known for two long-lasting publications.

- The **Pennsylvania Gazette**: Franklin took over the newspaper in 1729 and continued to write for it after he retired. Alongside the typical contents of a newspaper (see page 43), it also contained humorous letters written by Franklin, which helped it to sell.
- **Poor Richard's Almanack**: he produced numerous editions of this almanac* between 1732 and 1758. It contained useful information, such as a calendar and weather chart, as well as entertaining material, such as proverbs* and poems.

Key terms

Almanac*

A handbook of useful and practical information covering different subjects. Most homes of educated people in British America would have one.

Proverbs*

A short saying, which offers advice or summarises a truth based on experience or common sense.

Source D

Some examples of the proverbs from *Poor Richard's Almanack*. These helped the almanac to become extremely popular.

Eat to live, and not live to eat... Where there's marriage without love, there will be love without marriage... Necessity never made a good bargain... None preaches better than the ant, and she says nothing... A Penny saved is Twopence clear... When the well's dry we know the worth of water... The sleeping fox catches no poultry... Diligence is the mother of good luck... He that pursues two hares at once does not catch one and lets the other go... Haste makes waste... God helps them that help themselves.

Franklin's work as a writer was of great significance. Most households would own an almanac, and Franklin, despite competition, managed to sell over 250,000 copies of his. It helped him to grow wealthy, but also provided ordinary people with the practical information valued by Enlightenment thinkers. As a newspaper editor, he was able to publish this information on a weekly basis, but his role also gave him a powerful voice in Pennsylvania. He used this to advertise and encourage enthusiasm for a broad range of philanthropic* schemes (see below). In this way, he used his writing as a vehicle for change.

Key term

Philanthropic*

A wish to help others. Philanthropists often donated time and money to campaign for improvements and provide services or buildings for other people.

A philanthropist

Improvements to the community

One of Franklin's aims was to improve his local community, and he was prepared to give up his time to achieve this. His first major project tried to tackle the disorganised fire service in Philadelphia. In 1736, he set up the Union Fire Company, which provided fire insurance and set out how volunteers should fight fires. He built on his success in this venture to promote other projects to improve the city.

- **Street paving, cleaning and lighting:** he set up a scheme on his own street and then used his position in the Pennsylvania Assembly to expand its scope in 1750.
- **The police force:** he worked on a proposal to improve the city's watchmen. The Assembly approved it in 1752.

Improvements to education

Franklin's philanthropy also helped to spread new ideas through his work in education. In 1731, he set up the first subscription library. By the 1740s, the library contained a huge range of books, many written by Enlightenment authors. Franklin also tried to change the focus of university education and increase access to it, as he helped to set up the Academy of Philadelphia (University of Pennsylvania) between 1751 and 1755. He raised donations of £2,000 and assisted in the design of a new curriculum. His was one of the earliest colleges to provide lessons in a broad range of subjects; by 1775, 164 students had graduated with a bachelor's degree.

Helping disadvantaged groups

Another way that Franklin tried to help was to tackle problems faced by disadvantaged groups. For example, in 1751 he founded the city hospital in Philadelphia for sick poor people. He came up with the idea for a matching grant* and then helped to raise donations for the hospital. He also became a member of a group that wanted to improve the lives of black people. In 1760, he joined the Associates of Dr Bray, which campaigned for their schooling. In these ways he used his money, powerful position and new ideas to promote good causes.

Key term

Matching grant*

An agreement that the amount raised by public donation would be matched by the government.

Activities   ?

1   On a sheet of paper, put the question 'What made Benjamin Franklin an influential man?' in the centre. Around it put three titles in boxes: 'He had money', 'He had power' and 'He had new ideas'.

   a   Around each of the boxes add notes about each title.

   b   Draw arrows between the boxes. Write how they are linked together on the arrow: for example, 'He had new ideas' and 'He had power' could be linked by 'his power helped him to get support for his ideas'.

2   Explain, in no more than 150 words, what made Benjamin Franklin an influential man.

An intellectual

Franklin was an enthusiastic scientist who helped inspire others to experiment and invent. In 1743, he founded the American Philosophical Society, which had members from across British America. The Society exchanged letters, designed experiments and met together to discuss them. These discussions helped Franklin to develop his own theories, which had an international impact. For example, in 1751, he wrote *Experiments and Observations on Electricity*, which described his theory of electricity and a method of investigating it. This was translated into French and then, after encouragement from the French king, tested near Paris in 1752.

Source E

Benjamin West's painting, *Franklin Drawing Electricity from the Sky* (1805). Although not an accurate scientific representation, it shows Franklin's experiment to prove that lightning had electrical properties.

The results of Franklin's theories and experiments led to several new inventions. Some of those that had practical uses include:

- **the lightning rod** (1753), which helped to protect buildings from lightning damage
- **bifocal spectacles** (1784), which helped people who were both short- and long-sighted
- **the four-sided lamp**, which was used for street lighting because it was easier to clean than the round version.

Some of these inventions, such as the lightning rod, have had a long-lasting impact and continue to be used today.

Extend your knowledge

The lightning experiment

Benjamin Franklin designed an experiment to test whether lightning had electrical properties. In 1753, he used a kite with an iron point to attract lightning and capture electricity in a glass jar. The success of his experiment led him to suggest that an iron rod should be positioned on top of a tall building, with a wire that channelled the electricity from a lightning strike into the ground to improve safety.

How did Franklin's success as a writer help him with this experiment?

Exam-style question, Section A

Explain **two** consequences for the American colonists of Benjamin Franklin's work as a writer. **8 marks**

Exam tip

This question is asking you about consequence. A good answer will focus on the effects of Franklin's work as a writer, thinking about what difference it made to the lives of the colonists.

Summary

- The Great Awakening renewed enthusiasm for religion in New England and the middle colonies.
- The religious revivals also encouraged the religious conversion of black people and Native Americans.
- The Enlightenment encouraged the foundation of new schools and colleges and broadened the range of subjects on offer.
- The Enlightenment led to the growth of newspapers and public libraries.
- Benjamin Franklin was influenced by Enlightenment ideas and helped to develop and spread them.

Checkpoint

Strengthen

S1 Give examples of the effects the religious revivals had in the 1740s.

S2 In what ways did the Enlightenment affect British America?

S3 Describe the ways Benjamin Franklin improved colonial society.

Challenge

C1 The significance of the Great Awakening, the Enlightenment and Benjamin Franklin was not the same for everyone. Explain which individual or development might have been the most significant to:

  a a poor farmer in Pennsylvania

  b an educated townsman in Philadelphia

  c a church minister in New England.

C2 Reflect on your answers to C1. Can you identify one of them that affected all three types of people? Explain how greatly it affected each of them.

How confident do you feel about your answers to these questions? If you're not sure you answered them well, try the Activities on page 44, but put the Great Awakening or Benjamin Franklin in the first box.

2.2 War

- Understand the changing relations between the French, Native Americans and British during and after King George's War, 1744–48.
- Understand the events and consequences of the French and Indian War, 1754–63.
- Understand the significance of the Treaty of Paris, 1763, and the Royal Proclamation of 1763.

King George's War, 1744–48

In 1744, New France and British America went to war. Their main aims were to:

- take land from each other (see Figure 2.3)
- control access, by river, to the interior of North America
- dominate the profitable fur trade with the Native Americans in the Ohio Country (see Figure 2.4).

In order to achieve these goals, both sides had to build and defend remote forts (see Figure 2.3). They also had to try and get help from Native American tribes, who could provide an estimated 14,000 warriors familiar with fighting on North American terrain.

War against the French and Native Americans, 1744–47

In 1744, the French declared war on the British as part of a European conflict called the War of the Austrian Succession. The conflict spread into North America where it was called King George's War. At the start, the Native Americans supported the French. The British had tried to win a big group of Native Americans, the Iroquois, over to their cause, but this was not very successful. In June 1744, at a meeting with the British at Albany, the Iroquois agreed to stay out of the war, but they would not actively help the British. This put New France in a position of strength.

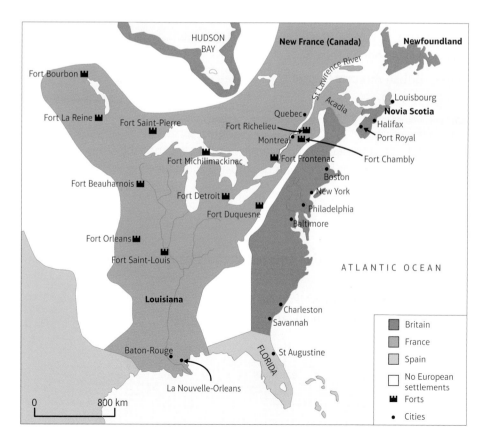

Figure 2.3 A map of the territories claimed by Britain and France and the boundary between them. It also shows the location of their forts, which were a long distance apart from each other.

48

The French used their advantage to strike the British first. In May 1744, the garrison* from the fort at Louisbourg attacked Canso, a British fishing village in Nova Scotia.

Key term

Garrison*

The troops who defend a fort or town.

Timeline

Key events in King George's War

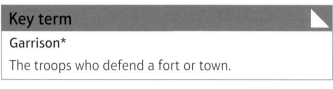

June 1745 The British capture the fort at Louisbourg from the French.

November 1745 300 French and 200 Native Americans attack Saratoga in New York. The British rebuild the fort afterwards.

June 1746 France sends a fleet of 65 ships to recapture Louisbourg, but it fails to reach its destination due to storm damage, an epidemic and the death of two French commanders.

January 1747 Joint force of French and Native Americans attacks Grand Pré, Nova Scotia, and the British surrender. The British retake it three months later.

June 1747 French and Native Americans capture Saratoga, but the British retake it and burn it down.

The New England colonists responded with an attack on Louisbourg, which was supported by Royal Navy ships from Britain. Even with Native American help, in June 1745, the French at Louisbourg had to surrender their fort. It was an important victory because Louisbourg was close to British territory and controlled access to French territory along the St Lawrence River (see Figure 2.3). However, it came at a cost. The French killed over 100 colonists during the siege and hundreds more died of disease while rebuilding the fort. Over the next two years, the fighting continued as the French and Native Americans raided British forts and settlements, but neither side made much progress (see timeline).

Improving relationships with the Native Americans, 1747–48

In April 1747, the Iroquois finally joined the British war effort and took part in an unsuccessful attempt to attack the French. Despite their failure, Native American support for the British grew stronger. At a meeting in Albany, New York in July 1748, the Iroquois agreed to launch a full-scale invasion of French Canada. However, before they had the opportunity to put this into practice, the British made peace with the French. The war was costing the British too much money and had made little progress in Europe and North America. As a result, the Treaty of Aix-la-Chapelle was signed in October 1748 and the war ended before the Native American alliance could make a difference.

Activities ?

1 Imagine you are the governor of Massachusetts and are preparing to speak to your colonial assembly. Write a few bullet-pointed notes you could use to respond to the following questions:

 a Why did you attack the French fort at Louisbourg?

 b What made you try to form an alliance with the Native Americans?

 c How are you going to try and convince Britain to keep control of Louisbourg?

2 Pair up with somebody else. One should be the governor, the other should represent the assembly. The assembly representative should ask the questions and challenge the governor on any points they feel the governor does not cover well enough.

3 Decide on a brief message to send to the British parliament before a treaty with the French is signed. Compare your idea with other members of the class.

Effects of King George's War

The Treaty of Aix-la-Chapelle ended the war in both the British Empire and in Europe. Under the treaty, Britain gave Louisbourg back to France, while France returned Madras in India to the British Empire. The treaty made the colonists feel:

- **abandoned**: in 1746, the British had promised to provide more troops and pay for an attack on Canada, but the plan was called off and no further help was sent to the colonies
- **angry**: Louisbourg was the only territory gained in King George's War and many died in the attempt. The colonists were furious that it was returned to the French for a territory thousands of miles away
- **disappointed**: the colonists had hoped to take land from the French and Spanish colonies in North America, but the treaty meant they had failed to achieve this aim.

Relationships after King George's War, 1748–53

The Treaty of Aix-la-Chapelle (1748) restored ownership of territory to the situation in 1744. As a result, neither side had achieved their original aims for the war. The British and French still wanted to control the Ohio Country (see Figure 2.4), while the Native Americans wanted to settle in it. This created a tense situation, which the British made worse through a series of actions in the late 1740s.

- Between 1747 and 1750, the British and colonial authorities gave out 1.3 million acres in land grants* to encourage settlement in the Ohio Country.
- In 1749, the British established a fur trading post at Pickawillany to compete with the French.
- In 1749, the British established a settlement at Halifax to rival the fort at Louisbourg.

Key term

Land grant*

Ownership rights to an area of land. A company or proprietor would be granted the land, often already used by Native Americans, and they would sell it to farmers or traders to settle on.

By the early 1750s, these measures had angered the Native Americans and threatened the French. The French responded with a new fort-building programme in the Ohio Country (see Figure 2.4) and an attack on Pickawillany. Some Native Americans helped the French to destroy this settlement and, in 1753, the Iroquois ended their alliance with the British. This put the British in a vulnerable situation, with two angry neighbours to their north and west who could block, or even reverse, their expansion.

Source A

An account written by a Native American ally of New France in 1754, giving his views about English and French colonists.

Brethren, are you ignorant of the difference between our Father [the French] and the English? Go see the forts our Father has erected, and you will see that the land beneath his walls is still hunting ground... whilst the English, on the contrary, no sooner get possession of a country than the game is forced to leave it; the trees fall down before them; the earth becomes bare, and we find among them hardly... [any means] to shelter us when the night falls.

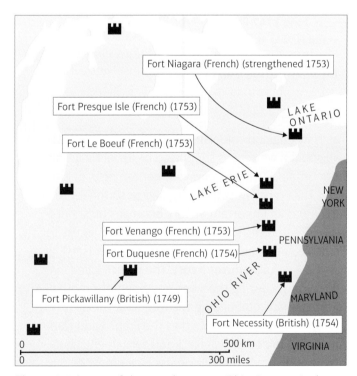

Figure 2.4 A map of the area known as Ohio Country. It shows the forts that the French and British built or strengthened after King George's War.

The French and Indian War (1754–63) in North America

War with the French, and their Native American allies, restarted when the British tried to end the French fort-building programme. In 1753, George Washington had been sent to warn the French to stop building Fort Duquesne (see Figure 2.4), but they ignored him. When Washington returned in May 1754 with Native American allies of his own, he attacked and killed a small group of French soldiers. In retaliation, the French forces from Fort Duquesne trapped Washington at Fort Necessity (see Figure 2.4) in July and killed or wounded a third of his forces. He was forced to surrender and the French and Indian War, which by 1756 had become part of the worldwide Seven Years' War, had begun.

At first, the British suffered a series of defeats. In July 1755, General Braddock tried to capture Fort Duquesne, but failed. Nine hundred of his troops were killed, in comparison to only 40 on the French side. The few Native Americans who still supported Britain then turned against them. Over the next two years, the Native Americans attacked the frontiers of British America and many settlers died. The British also began to lose control of their military posts, as their enemies captured Fort Oswego (1756) and Fort William Henry (1757). At this stage, it looked as though the French would win the war.

Extend your knowledge

The capture of Fort William Henry

The battle for Fort William Henry was a short one. The British surrendered after a few days and French General Montcalm offered them safe passage to Fort Edward. However, his Native American allies expected to take prisoners and scalps, the hair and skin covering the top of the head, which was removed from an enemy. Native American warriors expected to take scalps as a symbol of victory in battle. Montcalm attempted to stop them, but they still killed 200 and captured 300 British. His actions damaged relations with the Native Americans.

In what ways did this event affect French chances of victory in the war?

Impact of early defeats

In 1757, William Pitt became the British politician in charge of the war effort. His response to the earlier defeats in the war was to improve the British approach to the conflict. He:

- **raised more troops and supplies:** Pitt sent 8,000 British troops to the colonies and 12 warships. He also offered to pay the colonists for any troops they raised and gave them around £1 million (worth around £120 million today) for this
- **improved the quality of the leadership:** Pitt replaced an unsuccessful British commander-in-chief, Lord Loudoun, with a number of generals who reported to Pitt directly
- **tried to ease the tension between the British and colonial troops:** there had been arguments over rank in the army because a British lieutenant could outrank a colonial captain. Pitt took measures to improve the position of colonial officers.

Source B

An 18th-century painting of the fall of Louisbourg in 1758. It demonstrates how important British ships, in the foreground, were to the attack on the fortress town.

Success in North America

Pitt's measures helped to transform the situation in North America. In July 1758, the British recaptured the fort at Louisbourg (see Source B), which closed down the main route for French supplies (see Figure 2.5). France's position grew desperate when the British captured Fort Frontenac in August, which was packed with food stocks. With fewer supplies, the Native Americans began to desert the French. By November, there were so few allies left that the French commanding officer of Fort Duquesne decided to burn his fortress down rather than surrender it. When the British captured it shortly after, they built Fort Pitt on the site and secured control of the Ohio Country.

The role of Wolfe in Canada

By 1758, the French had withdrawn to their settlements in Canada. In order to defeat them, the British planned a campaign to capture the major forts and towns there. It began in June 1759, when General James Wolfe led a fleet of ships to Quebec, the capital of the French colonists. Once landed near the city, his forces fired their cannon into the city and burnt down the surrounding countryside. This carried on for two months, but Wolfe made little progress. He could not get past Quebec's defences, so instead he terrorised the population and tried to reduce the flow of supplies to the defenders.

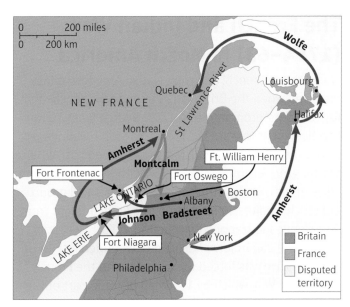

Figure 2.5 The French and Indian War in Canada.

He really wanted a traditional battle, where the two sides faced each other in open countryside, but General Montcalm had kept his forces behind Quebec's defensive walls and trenches.

In September 1759, Wolfe tried to tempt Montcalm into battle. He landed his army upstream of Quebec, tricked guards to let him pass, and took his forces up a rocky path onto the plains outside the city. Montcalm had assumed that no attack force would make it up the steep ground and so was not ready to defend this location.

Activity ?

Imagine you are a colonial soldier in July 1758. Write a letter to persuade a fellow colonist to join the war effort. You should refer to:

a the losses the colonists have suffered (use Figure 2.6).

b the help on offer from the British (look at Source B and re-read the information on William Pitt).

c the possible contribution the Native Americans could make if more joined your side.

Source C

A painting by Benjamin West, c1779, of the death of General Wolfe at Quebec.

Rather than prepare carefully, Montcalm sent his forces out hastily, in a poorly organised formation, and Wolfe got the traditional battle he wanted. The British fired disciplined volleys* at the approaching French forces, then charged at the enemy and defeated them. Wolfe, at the moment of his triumph, was killed in the battle and became a hero of the war.

The importance of General Wolfe

The battle for Quebec was over quickly because of Wolfe's preparations. In the lead up to it he had:

- **used terror to scare Quebec's population.** His forces had fired cannons at the residential area of the city for two months. As a consequence, many of its population wanted to surrender
- **destroyed the land around Quebec.** This, coupled with the loss of other French forts further south, made it difficult to get supplies into the city
- **trained his army well.** They knew how to fight a traditional pitched battle*, which helped them defeat the disorganised French forces outside Quebec.

Key terms

Volley*

A series of shots fired at the same time by a line of soldiers.

Pitched battle*

A battle where two sides decide to face one another. Each army would line up in regular formations, attack with both cannon and muskets, and organise charges against the other side.

French surrender

While Wolfe attacked Quebec, Pitt ordered his other generals to capture important French-controlled forts from the south. In July 1759, General Johnson, with help from Native Americans who had turned against the French, took the fort at Niagara. At the same time, General Amherst took advantage of Wolfe's attack on Quebec. He knew that most of the French forces would be helping Quebec, which meant their forts would be poorly defended. As a result, he was able to take two important forts in Canada without a fight.

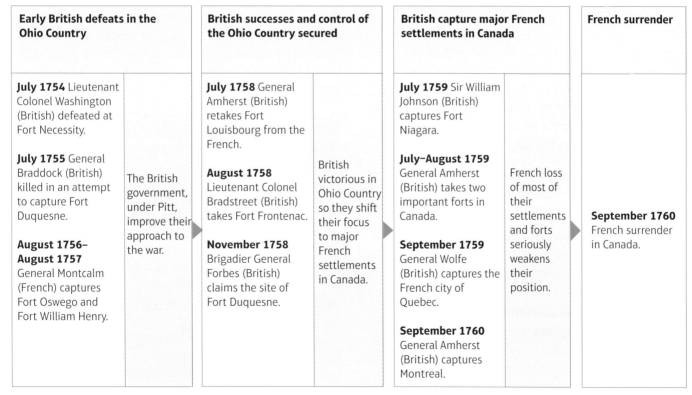

Early British defeats in the Ohio Country		British successes and control of the Ohio Country secured		British capture major French settlements in Canada		French surrender
July 1754 Lieutenant Colonel Washington (British) defeated at Fort Necessity. **July 1755** General Braddock (British) killed in an attempt to capture Fort Duquesne. **August 1756– August 1757** General Montcalm (French) captures Fort Oswego and Fort William Henry.	The British government, under Pitt, improve their approach to the war.	**July 1758** General Amherst (British) retakes Fort Louisbourg from the French. **August 1758** Lieutenant Colonel Bradstreet (British) takes Fort Frontenac. **November 1758** Brigadier General Forbes (British) claims the site of Fort Duquesne.	British victorious in Ohio Country so they shift their focus to major French settlements in Canada.	**July 1759** Sir William Johnson (British) captures Fort Niagara. **July–August 1759** General Amherst (British) takes two important forts in Canada. **September 1759** General Wolfe (British) captures the French city of Quebec. **September 1760** General Amherst (British) captures Montreal.	French loss of most of their settlements and forts seriously weakens their position.	**September 1760** French surrender in Canada.

Figure 2.6 Key stages in the French and Indian War.

By September 1760, all three British armies had taken important sites and had secured control of them. This freed them up for an attack on the last major French settlement at Montreal. Led by Amherst, the British forces took the city on 7 September 1760 and the French surrendered. Fighting continued elsewhere until 1762, but the conflict in British America and French Canada had achieved its final objective. As far as the colonists were concerned, the French and Indian War was over.

Exam-style question, Section A

Write a narrative account analysing the key events of 1758–60 that led to the French surrender.

You may use the following in your answer:

- the French abandon Fort Duquesne (1758)
- the capture of Montreal (1760).

You **must** also use information of your own. **8 marks**

Exam tip

This question targets your ability to write an analytical narrative. In your answer, consider the links between each event in the lead-up to the capture of Montreal.

Consequences of the French and Indian War

During the French and Indian War, the relationship between the colonists of British America and their mother country began to change. The war was a turning point partly because of the terms of the Treaty of Paris (see below) but also because of the effects it had on those that fought in it. The war:

- **unified the colonists:** the various immigrant groups fought together in colonial units, which helped to bond them together for the first time
- **gave many colonists training in warfare:** some soldiers who became significant in the American Revolution, such as George Washington, gained valuable experience from it
- **created tension between the colonial soldiers and the British regulars*:** the two sides argued over quartering* troops, over rank and sometimes struggled to work together as a team (see page 51)

- **damaged their economic relationship with Britain:** the war cost a huge amount. The British national debt rose from around £75 million at the start of the war to £122 million by the end. Britons had to pay heavy taxes as a result. In contrast, the colonists paid little in the way of taxation and avoided some customs duties through smuggling (see page 32).

The fighting had therefore strengthened colonial society and the confidence of the colonists, but placed considerable strain on their relationship with Britain.

Key terms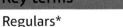

Regulars*

Professional soldiers who have a permanent job in an army.

Quartering*

Providing accommodation for troops. The British had the legal power to force inns and taverns to provide rooms for their soldiers.

The significance of the Treaty of Paris, 1763

The French and Indian War came to an end when the Treaty of Paris, which concluded the Seven Years' War, was signed in 1763. Its terms affected the French, the Spanish (who allied with France towards the end of the war) and the British. They are summarised in the table below.

Country	Gains
France	• Major sugar islands in the West Indies from Britain
	• Small fishing islands in Newfoundland from Britain
Spain	• Cuba from Britain
	• North America west of the Mississippi River from France
Britain	• Small islands in the West Indies from France
	• North America east of the Mississippi River (including Canada) from France
	• Florida from Spain

THINKING HISTORICALLY Cause and Consequence (2c)

Far-reaching consequences

Most events have multiple consequences. Their impact can often be felt in many different 'strands' of history, e.g. the Wall Street crash had economic consequences, but also affected society, politics and international relations. The French and Indian War between 1754 and 1763 was a significant event in the history of British America that had consequences in several different areas.

```
                   Event: the French and Indian War, 1754–63
```

| **Consequence:** the British took control of the Ohio Country from the French. | **Consequence:** the British secured control of the fur trade with the Native Americans. | **Consequence:** the British defeated the French in Canada. | **Consequence:** the war cost a lot of money and pushed up the British national debt. | **Consequence:** the fighting helped to unify the colonists. | **Consequence:** the war helped give the colonists training in warfare. |

1 How many consequences have been identified? Do you think this list is complete? If not, what has been missed?

2 Suggest a category (e.g. territorial, social, economic, etc.) for each consequence. How many categories have you ended up with?

3 Which of these consequences do you think the British might have had in mind when they decided to give their full support to the French and Indian War?

4 Which of the consequences might a historian writing a history of North America **not** refer to? Explain your answer.

5 Write one historical question about the French and Indian War that might require the historian to know about all these consequences in order to answer it well.

Source D

A map produced in 1763, which shows the distribution of land after the Treaty of Paris. Note that France gave the Louisiana territory (shown in yellow) to Spain (pink) as compensation for her losses to Britain (green).

Consequences of the treaty

The Treaty of Paris transformed North America because it meant the French Empire was no longer a powerful force there. It had a number of positive consequences for the British colonists, which included:

- **the removal of the French threat:** the colonists no longer had to worry about French-organised raids on their frontier settlements, or attacks on their forts
- **availability of land:** the colonists could begin to settle on land that was previously under French control
- **control of the fur trade:** the French abandoned their trading posts, which gave the colonists more control over the profitable fur trade with the Native Americans.

However, the benefits that the colonists enjoyed came at the cost of other groups, such as:

- **the mother country:** the removal of the French Empire from North America meant the colonists felt less dependent on Britain for protection. This made it more difficult to enforce new legislation and taxation on the colonists, because they did not see a need for it
- **the Native Americans:** they could no longer rely on the French to prevent British expansion into their lands. In addition, British colonists were now their only source of guns and ammunition. If a war broke out, they would struggle to find allies or weapons to prevent a British victory
- **the foreign colonists under British rule:** French colonists in Canada and Spanish colonists in Florida were now in British territories. Some fled, like the freed slaves at Mose (see page 26), who went to Cuba. Others stayed put, including the French in Canada, but became subject to British rule as a result.

Exam-style question, Section A

Explain **two** consequences of the Treaty of Paris (1763). **8 marks**

Exam tip

This question is asking you about consequence. It focuses on a treaty, so you should think about the way it affects different groups or countries.

The significance of the Royal Proclamation of 1763

In order to manage the new land British America gained in the Treaty of Paris and to improve relations with the Native Americans (see 'Pontiac's Rebellion' on page 62), King George III issued a Royal Proclamation on 7 October 1763. The Proclamation set up the colonies of Quebec, East Florida and West Florida as part of British America. It also fixed a Proclamation Line, which was a western boundary that followed the line of the Appalachian Mountains (see Figure 2.10). It also banned colonial settlement to the west of this point, and cancelled any land claims in Native American territory which had been made before the Proclamation, to prevent territorial disputes with the Native Americans.

The impact of the Royal Proclamation of 1763

The Proclamation had a number of positive consequences, which included:

- **improved British relations with the Native Americans:** the Ohio Country was now reserved for the Native Americans, and two superintendents* were appointed to manage relations with them
- **increased trade with the Native Americans:** it removed the limit on the number of trading licences which could be granted to those who traded with Native Americans
- **the encouragement of settlement in the new colonies:** the governors of Quebec, East Florida and West Florida could grant free land to soldiers who had fought in the French and Indian War.

However, the significance of the Proclamation was limited by the problems it caused. These are outlined in the diagram on page 57.

Key term

Superintendent*

The head of a department. The Indian Superintendent controlled relations between the Native Americans and British traders and settlers.

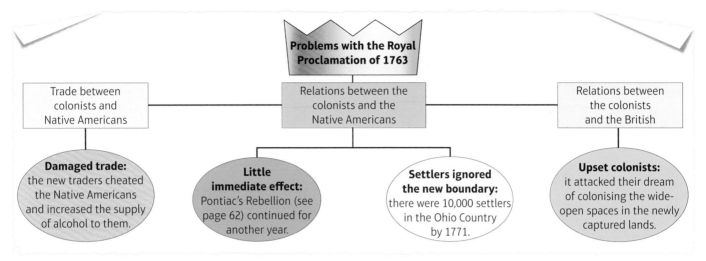

Figure 2.7 The impact of the Royal Proclamation of 1763.

Summary

- The British fought the French and their Native American allies during King George's War (1744–48).
- After the war, colonists angered the Native Americans and the French as they expanded into the Ohio Country.
- British forces suffered defeats in the French and Indian War (1754–63) until William Pitt became prime minister.
- Britain took control of the Ohio Country with the capture of Fort Duquesne in 1758.
- General Wolfe played a central role in the capture of Quebec (1759), which led to the end of the war in Canada.
- The Treaty of Paris (1763) gave Britain control of a huge area of North America and Canada.
- The Royal Proclamation of 1763 established a boundary between British America and Native American territory.

Checkpoint

Strengthen

S1 Identify three ways in which the British damaged their relationship with the French and the Native Americans between 1744 and 1753.

S2 Summarise the main events in the French and Indian War (1754–63).

S3 What facts or events show that the relationship between British America and the mother country had weakened as a result of the French and Indian War?

Challenge

C1 An event in a war can be significant because it changes the unfolding situation in a number of ways. Find and explain an event in King George's War or the French and Indian War that:

    a significantly improved the British chance of victory   **b** removed an obstacle to victory

    c inspired a greater number of people to commit to the war effort.

C2 Choose an event in the French and Indian War you think is the most significant. Explain your reasoning.

C3 How would you rate the significance of the Treaty of Paris? Explain your answer with reference to the different groups it had an effect on.

How confident do you feel about your answers to these questions? If you're not sure you answered them well, put each event into a table with two columns headed 'Event' and 'Effect'. List one effect for the colonists of each event.

2.3 The aftermath of the war

Learning outcomes

- Understand the impact of the French and Indian War on relations with Britain.
- Understand the key features of the Sugar Act of 1764 and the colonists' opposition to it.
- Understand the effects of Pontiac's Rebellion and the actions of the Paxton Boys on relations with the Native Americans.

The impact of the war on relations with Britain

Victory in the French and Indian War was a result of the combined effort of British and colonial troops. They had removed the threat of the French Empire and secured control of the east coast of North America. Despite this success, the close contact between them in the war had weakened their relations in a number of ways.

Damage to personal relations

During the war, the British sent over generals from an aristocratic background and highly trained and disciplined regular soldiers. In contrast, the colonial generals had little formal training and relied on locally organised militia forces. The effects were:

- the British thought that the colonists were poor soldiers and were too keen to go home because of the low pay offered for military service
- the colonists felt the British were too harsh in the treatment of their troops.

This resulted in ill feeling between the two sides, which was worsened by the actions of some British generals. For example, Lord Loudoun had decided to quarter his troops in private homes, which infuriated the colonists. The situation did improve once Pitt came to power, but the regular soldiers and colonial militia never truly got along with each other.

Damage to economic relations

The cost of the war placed a big strain on economic relations between Britain and the American colonies. Once it was over, the British government realised they would have to pay for a standing army in North America to defend the frontier (see 'Impact of Pontiac's Rebellion' on page 63). British residents paid taxes of up to 18 shillings (£120) per person, which were used to help fund this defence, whereas the colonists only paid taxes of up to 4 shillings (£25). As a result, British taxpayers began to resent the colonists and the British government looked for ways to get them to pay for their own defence (see 'The Sugar Act, 1764' on page 60).

The British were even angrier when they realised that, instead of helping to pay off war debts, the colonists had increased their smuggling activities. For example, they smuggled goods to the French West Indies. Not only was trade with the French colonies illegal after 1756, but also it affected the amount of customs revenue the British collected. The colonists did not pay customs duties on goods they smuggled and so avoided them altogether.

Damage to political relations

The war also increased the boldness of the colonial assemblies*, which began to take actions that the British government did not approve of. They used the opportunity of a temporary wartime emergency to:

- **increase their control of the economy:** colonial assemblies ignored British currency rules and began to print more paper money*
- **attempt to take control of the legal system:** some colonies planned to pay judges from their own funds and therefore remove their dependence on Britain.

Key terms

Colonial assembly*

A form of government in which a group of leading individuals represented their colony.

Paper money*

Currency issued by a government in paper form.

Even though the British authorities put a stop to both of these measures, the actions of the colonial assemblies demonstrate their growing confidence to challenge the British government.

Source A

An example of a five pound note that was produced in New York in 1759, during the French and Indian War. It was issued by the colonial assembly.

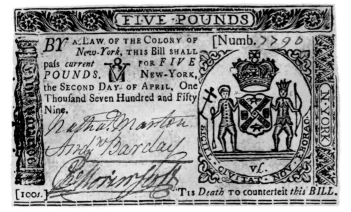

Activities ?

The colonist in Figure 2.8 summarises the attitude many had towards their mother country in 1763. However, the British, who had paid for, planned and fought the war, did not agree with them. Consider this when approaching the activities below.

1. Imagine it is 1763. Write a short diary entry that describes your attitude to the colonists from the point of view of one of the following:

   a a British general who fought alongside colonial troops

   b the prime minister of Britain

   c a British captain in the Royal Navy.

2. Work in groups of students who have written from different points of view. Discuss whether there are any common themes in your entries.

3. Imagine a colonist has found your diary entry. Annotate it with how he or she would respond to the criticisms in it.

Extend your knowledge

The Currency Act, 1764

Between 1754 and 1764, the amount of paper money printed in the colonies grew by 355%. This was a problem because it was used to pay off British merchants but quickly lost its value. In 1764, parliament put a stop to this and issued the Currency Act, which banned the printing of paper money in the colonies. Metal coins were worth their weight in the precious metal they were made of, so their value did not change. However, there were not enough metal coins in circulation to replace the paper money, so colonial trade was damaged because it was difficult to pay for goods and pay off debts.

Can you connect the French and Indian War to the passing of the Currency Act?

Figure 2.8 The impact of the French and Indian War on relations with Britain.

Opposition to the Sugar Act

The Sugar Act, 1764

On 5 April 1764, parliament passed the Sugar Act, which was Britain's first attempt to try to take control of economic relations with the North American colonies. The Act was designed to raise a large sum of money from the colonists and use it to pay off the war debt. Its main terms changed the rules set out under the Molasses Act of 1733 (see page 14).

- **A reduction of the tax on foreign molasses from 6 pence to 3 pence per gallon:** this encouraged traders to pay the tax, rather than bribe customs collectors to let them smuggle their goods in.
- **An increase in the tax on foreign sugar that had been processed:** the tax was raised on foreign refined sugar and the import of foreign rum was banned.
- **Payment of the tax had to be in metal coinage:** colonists were prevented from using their own paper money, which had a lower value than metal coins.
- **Measures to stop smuggling:** a vice-admiralty court was set up at Halifax to try smugglers. Also, traders had to get paperwork from the nearest customs office before they shipped certain goods listed in the Act.

Effects of the Sugar Act

The colonists saw the Sugar Act as a threat because it was actively enforced and ended a period of 'salutary neglect'* that had begun in 1721. Now, any customs officer who had avoided their duties and stayed in England was ordered to return to their job in the colonies full time.

Key term
Salutary neglect* The unofficial policy that colonies were allowed to run their own government and economy with limited interference from the British government. Trade laws were also weakly enforced, which allowed the colonial economy to thrive.

In addition, the Royal Navy sent out 20 ships to find smugglers, who would then be placed on trial in a vice-admiralty court. These courts were seen as unfair because they did not have a jury and the judge received 5% of any smuggled cargo. In such a court, the decision was in the hands of a judge, who was more likely to find a smuggler guilty in order to collect his share.

Finally, the Sugar Act attempted to limit trade with the foreign colonies in the West Indies, which had provided the colonists with foreign metal coins. The effect of the Act was to reduce, but not entirely stop, this trade and lower the amount of metal coinage in British America. Without these coins, colonists struggled to pay their taxes and settle their debts.

Responses to the Sugar Act

A year before the Sugar Act was introduced, the colonists had found out about the plans for it through their London contacts. In April 1763, Boston's merchants set up the Society for Encouraging Trade and Commerce to defend against any new trade laws. When the Sugar Act was finally introduced, this group, along with similar ones from other colonies, used various methods to challenge it. The diagram below shows some of these different methods.

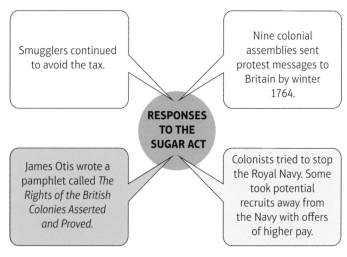

Figure 2.9 Responses to the Sugar Act of 1764.

Source B

From an influential pamphlet by James Otis, a politician in Massachusetts, called *The Rights of the British Colonies Asserted and Proved*. It was published in Boston in 1764 as a response to the Sugar Act.

The colonists, being men, have a right to be considered as equally entitled to all the rights of nature with the Europeans, and they are not to be restrained in the exercise of any of these rights but for the evident good of the whole community. By being or becoming members of society they have not renounced their natural liberty in any greater degree than other good citizens, and if 'tis taken from them without their consent they are so far enslaved.

Impact of opposition

Parliament had hoped to collect £78,000 per year from the Sugar Act. However, the opposition in British America meant that little tax was collected. It was only when the tax was dropped from 3 pence to 1 penny per gallon of molasses in 1766 that the colonists finally began to pay it. Their actions had shown that if parliament tried to raise money without agreement from the colonial assemblies, the customs officers would struggle to collect it.

Exam-style question, Section A

Explain **two** of the following:

- The importance of William Pitt's appointment as prime minister in 1757 for the British victory in the French and Indian War
- The importance of the Treaty of Paris of 1763 for the colonists in British America
- The importance of the Sugar Act of 1764 for relations between Britain and its North American colonies. **16 marks**

Exam tip

This question targets your ability to explain the importance of a development or individual. A good answer will choose detail to show that it had a clear effect on the development or situation.

Activity

Divide into two groups. One represents the colonies and the other represents the mother country. Debate the view that the colonists should obey the terms of the Sugar Act of 1764.

Relations with the Native Americans

Relations between the Native Americans and the colonists worsened at the end of the French and Indian War. Without a French threat, the colonists no longer felt they needed to keep on good terms with the Native Americans. As a result, General Amherst stopped the policy of gift giving* to them and limited the goods they could trade for. The effect was to cut off Native American supplies of ammunition, which they had come to rely on for hunting and warfare.

Key term

Gift giving*

The practice of giving presents to an ally. The British gave the Native Americans gifts like alcohol, muskets and ammunition to maintain good military and trade relations.

The British also began to break previous agreements with the Native Americans, by:

- **keeping troops at the forts and trading posts they had captured**, even at those they had agreed to leave
- **allowing settlers to spread into the land of allied Native Americans**. Before the Royal Proclamation was issued in October 1763 (see page 56), this was a serious problem in the Ohio Country and in Carolina's frontier region.

These actions worried Native Americans, who had lost their French ally and now depended on the British as their only source for good-quality European goods.

Pontiac's Rebellion, 1763–66

On 27 April 1763, a council of around 400 Native Americans, under the leadership of a war chief called Pontiac, set up an alliance between most of the northern tribes. The following month they began to attack the British and, by the end of the year, had managed to capture all the British forts and posts in the Ohio Country, except for Detroit, Fort Pitt and Fort Niagara. They had also attacked frontier settlements and killed over 2,000 colonists and 400 soldiers.

The British response

The attacks in the Ohio Country had come as a surprise to the British. However, by mid-1763 they had begun to resist the Native Americans successfully. One strategy the British used involved germ warfare. In June 1763, blankets and a handkerchief infected with smallpox were given to the Native Americans during negotiations over Fort Pitt. The disease spread rapidly, but the siege on Fort Pitt continued. It was not until the Battle of Bushy Run that Fort Pitt was rescued from its attackers and, by September, two tribes returned to their alliance with the British. The rebellion continued until Pontiac signed a peace treaty in 1766.

Timeline
Pontiac's Rebellion

27 April 1763 Pontiac helps to create an alliance between most northern Native American tribes.

9 May 1763 Pontiac begins to attack Detroit and other British forts and trading posts.

31 July 1763 Native Americans ambush British troops at Bloody Run, near Detroit, killing 21 of them.

5 August 1763 British rescue Fort Pitt at the Battle of Bushy Run.

14 September 1763 The Devil's Hole Massacre: Native Americans attack at Devil's Hole, Niagara, killing 73 British troops.

7 September 1764 After a British invasion of the Ohio Country, several tribes sign the Detroit Treaty.

October 1763 Royal Proclamation issued.

July 1766 Pontiac finally agrees to peace with the Indian superintendent, Sir William Johnson.

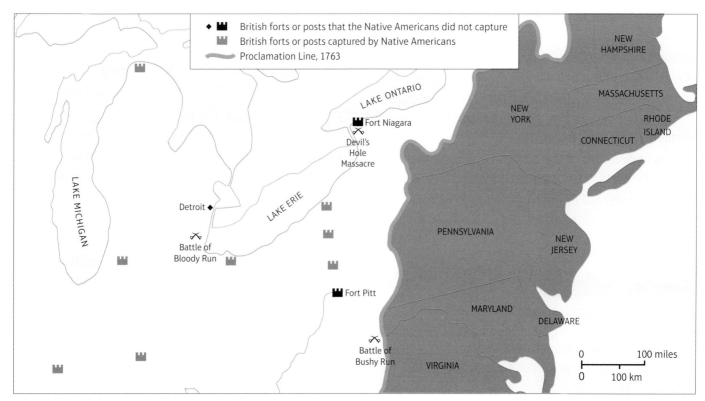

Figure 2.10 The main events of Pontiac's Rebellion, 1763–66.

Impact of Pontiac's Rebellion

Pontiac's Rebellion had a big impact on the British treatment of the Native Americans. General Amherst had wanted to destroy them, but the British government wanted to prevent future rebellions. In order to minimise the threat from them, the British:

- renewed their policy of gift giving to the Native Americans and lifted trade restrictions
- issued the Proclamation of 1763, which limited how far west colonists could settle (see page 56)
- decided to leave 10,000 British troops in the colonies, increasing running costs to £440,000 per year.

These actions improved relations between the British and Native Americans but damaged their relations with the colonists. The British were angry with the colonists, who they believed had done little to defend themselves during the rebellion. On the other hand, colonists on the frontier were annoyed by the limits placed on the expansion of their settlements and the presence of British regulars, who could be used against them (see opposite).

Interpretation 1

An extract from the book *The Scratch of a Pen 1763 and the Transformation of North America* by Colin Calloway, published in 2006. It explores the impact of Pontiac's Rebellion on relations with the Native Americans.

The Indians did not win the war of 1763, but they asserted their power and wrung some concessions from the greatest empire in the world. The British demanded rights to the posts they had taken from the French, rights of free passage through Indian country, the return of prisoners, and hostages as a guarantee that the terms would be met. The British stepped back from Amherst's insistence on treating Indians as a conquered people. Instead, they stepped into the role of 'fathers' formerly occupied by the French and learned to deal with the Indians as allies.

The Paxton Boys: their actions

Stage 1: the massacre in Lancaster

The Paxton Boys was a militia unit made up of Scots-Irish frontier settlers. It was set up in Pennsylvania in July 1763 as part of a small effort by the colonists to fight against Pontiac's Rebellion. However, the Paxton Boys had grown angry because of the limited help they had received from the Pennsylvania authorities to protect the colonists.

By the end of July, there was a serious refugee problem in Pennsylvania as 1,384 frontier settlers abandoned their farms. In response to this, the Paxton Boys took extreme action. They mistakenly believed that the Conestoga Native Americans had helped their enemies and decided to attack them in December 1763. Fifty-seven Paxton Boys killed six peaceful Conestoga and then journeyed to Lancaster jail to murder another 14 who had taken shelter there.

Stage 2: the march on Philadelphia

As the danger to Native Americans increased in late 1763, 140 of them, who were mostly converts to Christianity, headed to Philadelphia for their own protection. In early 1764, the governor of Pennsylvania appealed for British help and British troops were placed in Lancaster and Philadelphia to defend against the Paxton Boys. However, the Paxton Boys had attracted 250 frontier settlers to their cause and in February 1764 marched to Philadelphia to kill the Native Americans.

On their journey to Philadelphia, the Paxton Boys stopped at Germantown and met with important politicians from Pennsylvania, led by Benjamin Franklin. They were presented with a generous offer. In return for not attacking the Native Americans, the Paxton Boys were promised greater protective measures on the frontier and offered an amnesty for their murders. The uprising came to an end, as they agreed to these terms and began to return home.

The Paxton Boys: their impact

In many ways the Paxton Boys were successful. They had got away with murdering innocent Native Americans and had received greater support from their colonial assembly for the frontier settlers. However, their success had a number of serious consequences.

- It made peace talks between members of Pontiac's Rebellion and the colonists more difficult.
- It made the Pennsylvania Assembly look weak, as they could not control their frontier settlers.

All of these consequences demonstrated that the Proclamation of 1763 was ineffective. The Pennsylvania Assembly had failed to punish the leaders of the Paxton Boys, which increased the confidence of the frontier settlers. They knew they could settle in the west without consequence. However, when they did so, relations with the Native Americans were at risk.

Exam-style question, Section A

Write a narrative account analysing the key events of Pontiac's Rebellion, 1763–66.

You may use the following in your answer:

- Native American fears
- Devil's Hole Massacre, 1763.

You **must** also use information of your own. **8 marks**

Exam tip

This question targets your ability to write an analytical narrative. Make sure the narrative has events in the correct sequence, with a clear beginning and outcome.

Summary

- The French and Indian War (1754–63) damaged relations between British America and the mother country.
- The Sugar Act (1764) was the first attempt to raise money from the colonists to help pay off the national debt.
- The colonists used a range of methods to oppose the Sugar Act.
- Pontiac's Rebellion (1763–66) led to the capture of British forts and the death of frontier settlers.
- The actions of the Paxton Boys (1763–64) led to the death of peaceful Native Americans and an increase in illegal settlement on Native American land.

Checkpoint

Strengthen

S1 Describe, in detail, three ways in which relations between the American colonists and Britain worsened as a result of the French and Indian War.

S2 What facts or ideas show that the colonists opposed the Sugar Act?

S3 What were the main events that affected British and Native American relations between 1763 and 1764?

Challenge

C1 Each of these developments has a long-term consequence in this part of the chapter. Identify a consequence and explain the connection with each of these developments:

   a the migration of Scots-Irish settlers to the frontier of Pennsylvania in the first half of the 18th century (see page 11)

   b the absence of any successful attempt to tax the colonists heavily between 1713 and 1741 (see page 32)

   c the problem of smuggling after the Molasses Act of 1733 (see page 33).

C2 Pick one answer to C1. Identify and explain another development that led to the same consequence. Explain how it did so.

How confident do you feel about your answers to these questions? If you're not sure you answered them well, try the task in reverse. Look for the long-term causes of three events or developments in this part of the chapter.

Recap: A disrupted society, 1742–64

Recall quiz

Have a go at these 10 quick-fire questions:

1 What religious movement reached a high point in the 1740s?

2 Which town had four newspapers by 1760?

3 Give one example of Benjamin Franklin's philanthropy.

4 When did the British colonists first capture the fort at Louisbourg from the French?

5 Over what area did the British, French and Native Americans fight for control until 1758?

6 Identify one economic consequence of the French and Indian War.

7 Name the treaty that ended the French and Indian War in 1763.

8 Which empire was removed from North America after the French and Indian War?

9 By how much did the tax on molasses fall under the Sugar Act?

10 In what year did both Pontiac's Rebellion and the forming of the Paxton Boys begin?

Exam-style question, Section A

Explain **two** of the following:

- The importance of Benjamin Franklin for intellectual developments in British America
- The importance of the Treaty of Aix-la-Chapelle (1748) for relations between the British colonists and the French in the years 1748–53
- The importance of Pontiac's Rebellion (1763–66) for British attitudes to the Native Americans.

16 marks

Exam tip

This question targets your ability to explain the importance of an individual, development or event. Focus your answer on how the situation changed as a result.

Activities

1 Copy and complete the table below:

In 1742	In 1764
Relations between the American colonists and the British were…	Relations between the American colonists and the British were…
The British controlled land in…	The British controlled more territory, which included…
The French threatened the colonists because…	The French no longer threatened the colonists because…
The colonists felt dependent on Britain because…	The colonists had grown in confidence because…
The British had not asked the colonists to pay much…	The British tried to raise money from the colonists by…
The colonists' relations with the Native Americans were…	The colonists' relations with the Native Americans were still…

2 Use the information in this chapter to complete the tasks below.

a Make notes in a table with the following headings: 'Cultural changes', 'Geographical changes' and 'Economic changes'.

b Explain why a strong relationship with the Native Americans was vital to success for a European colony in North America.

c Explain, in one paragraph, how the relationship between the North American colonists and Britain in 1764 compared with their relationship in 1713.

Writing historically: linking information

When you explain events and their consequences, you need to show how your ideas link together.

Learning outcomes

By the end of this lesson, you will understand how to:

- link ideas clearly and concisely using present participles and non-finite clauses.

Definitions

Non-finite clause: a clause beginning with a non-finite verb. These can be any of the below.

A present participle: a verb form ending in –ing, e.g. 'running', 'building', 'forming', 'falling', etc.

A past participle: a verb form often ending in –ed, e.g. 'formed', 'happened', etc, although there are several exceptions, e.g. 'ran', 'built', 'fell', etc.

An infinitive: the 'root' verb form, which often begins with 'to', e.g. 'to run', 'to build', 'to form', etc.

How can I link ideas using present participles?

You can structure sentences to link related ideas in a number of different ways. One way is to use a **present participle** to create a **non-finite clause**.

For example, look at all the different ways in which two sentences in the example answer below can be linked to this exam-style question:

> Explain **two** consequences of the Royal Proclamation of 1763 for relations between the British colonists and the Native Americans. **(8 marks)**

The Proclamation removed the limit on the number of licences for trade with Native Americans.	+ It increased the amount of trade.	=

The Proclamation removed the limit on the number of licences for trade with Native Americans, *increasing* the amount of trade.

This present participle clearly and succinctly links the two points together.

1. Look at the sentences below. How could you link them using a present participle?

The Proclamation reserved the Ohio Country for the Native Americans and appointed two superintendents to manage relations with them.	+ This reduced tensions.	=?
Despite the Proclamation, thousands of settlers ignored the new boundary and built farms in the Ohio Country.	+ This increased tensions with the Native Americans.	=?

2. a. Choose **either** of the sentences above. How else could you link them? Experiment with two or three different ways.

   b. Which of your experiments expresses the information most clearly? Write a sentence explaining your choice.

How can I link ideas using other kinds of non-finite verbs?

There are three forms of non-finite verb:

- Infinitives (e.g. 'to open', 'to make', 'to mean')
- Past participles (e.g. 'opened', 'made', 'meant')
- Present participles (e.g. 'opening', 'making', 'meaning')

Compare the sentences in the two examples below:

> The Royal Proclamation was issued in 1763. The Proclamation was an attempt to manage new land in British America and improve relations with the Native Americans.

This non-finite clause allows the writer to connect these two points much more neatly.

> Issued in 1763, the Royal Proclamation was an attempt to manage new land in British America and improve relations with the Native Americans.

Now compare these sentences in the two examples below:

> The government cancelled land claims in Native American territory. This was so it could prevent territorial disputes and outbreaks of violence.

This non-finite verb allows the writer to connect these two points much more neatly.

> The government cancelled land claims in Native American territory to prevent territorial disputes and outbreaks of violence.

3. Write as many sentences as you can linking these points using non-finite verbs.

> Merchants could easily obtain trading licences.   This increased the supply of furs.
>
> These allowed trade with the Native Americans.

Did you notice?

4. Non-finite clauses can often be positioned at different points in a sentence without affecting its meaning. Experiment with one or two of the sentences above, trying the non-finite clause in different positions.

Improving an answer

5. Look at the points noted below in response to this exam-style question:

> ```
> Explain the importance for the American colonists of Benjamin Franklin's
> work as a writer.
> ``` **(8 marks)**

> Franklin was a newspaper editor and wrote Poor Richard's Almanack.
>
> His publications contained practical information.

> His almanac sold over 250,000 copies.
>
> It helped to spread new ideas.
>
> He wrote about philanthropic schemes.

a. Experiment with different ways of linking some or all of the points using non-finite verbs.

b. Look carefully at all of the sentences you have written. Which ones work well, clearly and briefly linking ideas? Which do not? Use your findings to write a final redraft of the notes above, aiming to make your sentences as clear and concise as possible.

03 | The loss of an empire, 1765–83

In 1765, George Washington had gained fame in Virginia as a colonel who had fought alongside the British in the French and Indian War. At the same time, Thomas Jefferson had just finished his studies and begun a career that would see him become a well-known Virginian lawyer and a wealthy slave owner. Further north, Benjamin Franklin had just taken up a job as agent for Pennsylvania in London. At the start of their careers, all three were loyal men who were subjects of the British Empire and benefited from their part in it.

However, in just under 30 years, their lives had been transformed from colonial celebrities to national heroes. Washington had led a rebel army that had forced the British into a humiliating surrender at Yorktown in 1781. Jefferson had drafted the Declaration of Independence in 1776, which broke the ties between the colonies and the mother country. And Franklin had taken the lead in peace negotiations that forced the British to recognise the new United States of America as a free and independent nation. In 1783, the stories of these three men were the stories of a new nation. That nation was born out of a conflict that lasted eight years, involved three European powers and called upon the support of 375,000 rebels.

Learning outcomes

By the end of this chapter, you will understand:

- the significance of British policies, and the reaction to them in the colonies, in causing the American decision to rebel
- the major events, individuals and developments that contributed to the achievement of independence for the United States of America in 1783
- the consequences of the War of Independence for slaves, Native Americans and loyalists.

Learning outcomes

- Understand the significance of the Stamp Act and the impact of the groups who opposed the act, including the Sons of Liberty.
- Understand the events of the Boston Massacre and the Boston Tea Party, as well as the British reaction to them.
- Understand the significance of the First and Second Continental Congresses in the lead up to the outbreak of the War of Independence.

The significance of British policies

After the Sugar Act of 1764 (see page 60), the American colonists were increasingly worried that, if parliament began to tax them successfully, more and more taxes would be introduced. In the late 1760s, three Acts were passed in parliament, which the colonists saw as an attempt to raise money from them and limit their freedom. The table below summarises them.

The Stamp Act caused widespread opposition in the colonies because, in the past, the British government had only taxed trade, but now the colonists were being taxed at home. The Act was seen as a threat to free speech and the sharing of information, as it taxed items including newspapers and almanacs. It also created fear amongst the colonists that they would lose their legal rights because it bypassed the colonial courts. The colonists' reaction was to challenge the authority of the British government. This helped to reverse some of these policies. The diagram on page 70 shows how the colonists responded to these measures.

Extend your knowledge

No taxation without representation
The colonists had no representatives in the British parliament and so believed it had no right to tax them. However, they did not want any members of parliament (MPs) because they thought that their own MPs could be outvoted. Instead, they wanted the right for their own colonial assemblies to organise taxation.

How significant do you think this argument was in the colonists' decision to oppose the Stamp Act?

Act	Key terms
Stamp Act of 1765	• A huge range of documents had to be printed on stamped paper and paid for by a tax. This included newspapers, insurance policies and even playing cards. • The tax had to be paid in British metal coinage, which was in short supply. • Law-breakers were to be tried in a vice-admiralty court, normally used for trying shipping cases. Three more were set up to help enforce the Act.
Quartering Act of 1765	• Colonists had to provide barracks for British troops and pay for their supplies. • Troops could be housed in inns and empty buildings without the owner's consent.
Revenue Act of 1767 (Townshend duties)	• New duties were placed on tea, glass, paper and painters' colours. • The duties would be used to pay the salaries of royal government representatives, such as judges and other officials. • A Board of Customs Commissioners was set up in Boston to oversee the collection of duties.

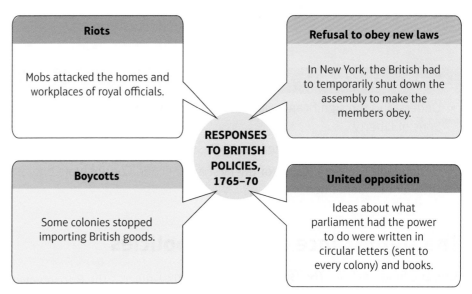

Figure 3.1 The responses to British policies in the 1760s.

American opposition to the Stamp Act of 1765

Before the legislation even came into force, the opponents of the Stamp Act took strong action. A group called the Sons of Liberty (see page 71) organised demonstrations and riots, merchants set up boycotts* of British goods and the colonial assemblies presented their objections to parliament. As a result, the British failed to collect the £60,000 per year that they had expected from the tax.

The political reaction

The first group to react were the politicians, because they were merchants, lawyers and other professionals, so the Stamp Act would have a huge effect on them. On 29 May 1765, the Virginia Assembly passed four resolutions. These became known as the Virginia Stamp Act Resolves, and they included the argument that the colonists could only be taxed if they were properly represented in the government that raised the taxes. This was the first step taken by a colonial government to protest against the Stamp Act. It was followed by a meeting of nine colonies, in October 1765, called the Stamp Act Congress. Although this meeting only resulted in an agreed set of objections to the Act, it was significant because it showed the colonists had begun to unite over their opposition to parliament.

Economic boycotts

As politicians debated their reaction to the Stamp Act, leading merchants decided to take their own action. From October 1765 onwards, New York City, then Philadelphia and later Boston, decided to boycott British goods and refused to pay off their debts to British traders. Back in Britain, traders in the major port cities of London, Liverpool and Bristol began to suffer.

Key term

Boycott*

An agreement not to import or purchase a certain type of goods, or import goods from another country. The colonists used boycotts as a tool to resist new British taxes.

They turned to parliament for help and petitioned the government to repeal (cancel) the Stamp Act in order to restore trade relations.

Mob action

At around the same time that the politicians and merchants organised their opposition, a much wider group of colonists began a series of violent protests. Mobs from across British America followed the lead of Boston's colonists. It was there that a skilled workers' club called the Loyal Nine, with the support of poor labourers, threatened a stamp tax collector, Andrew Oliver. On 14 August 1765, the demonstrators hung an effigy* of Oliver, then marched it around the city, burned it outside his house and smashed in his windows. The following day, he resigned as stamp tax collector. Rioting had proved effective in Boston and it quickly spread throughout the colonies thanks to the Sons of Liberty.

Spreading resistance: the Sons of Liberty

The first group to call themselves the Sons of Liberty was formed in New York in November 1765. It was made up of lawyers, skilled workers and merchants who wanted to resist the Stamp Act. They set up a committee to write letters to other colonies in order to spread their organisation, and they achieved rapid results. In Boston, the Loyal Nine changed their name to the Sons of Liberty and, by March 1766, groups had been established in the southern colonies as well.

The Sons of Liberty were very successful and by October 1766 they began to shut down their operations. Due to their work, no stamp tax collector took up his new job, except for a short time in Georgia, and only £3,292 was collected. They had shown that the British parliament could be resisted by effective communication, organised action and the power of local politics.

The impact of opposition

American opposition to the Stamp Act was so effective that the British government was forced to back down. The actions of the colonists ensured that:

- **there were no stamp tax collectors:** when the Act came into force on 1 November 1765, only one colony had a collector. He was forced to resign shortly after.
- **the Stamp Act was repealed:** in March 1766, parliament repealed the Stamp Act, although they replaced it with a Declaratory Act that confirmed parliament's power to make laws in British America
- **the colonists' interests were considered:** parliament passed the Free Port Act in 1766, which encouraged trade with the Spanish in the West Indies, where traders would be able to earn metal coins.

Key term

Effigy*
A model of a person. Rioters sometimes created a model of an unpopular figure so that they could attack it, hang it or burn it in order to intimidate the individual.

Exam-style question, Section A

Explain **two** consequences of the Stamp Act (1765). **8 marks**

Exam tip

This question is asking you about consequence. Try to consider the impact the Act had on both the colonists and on Britain.

It was a meeting point for colonists

In the summer of 1766, New Yorkers met at their liberty pole every day to discuss politics and practise military exercises.

It caused conflict

The British tried to pull down the liberty pole several times. On 13 January 1777, this led to a fight called the Battle of Golden Hill, which lasted two days.

It spread throughout the colonies

Many people copied New York City. Liberty poles were constructed in the middle colonies and in New England.

It was a deliberate challenge to the British authorities

The pole stood outside the Upper Barracks, which was garrisoned by British troops.

Figure 3.2 The significance of the New York liberty pole.

The liberty pole

On 21 May 1766, the colonists of New York City were celebrating the repeal of the Stamp Act. As part of their celebrations, they constructed a liberty pole, to serve as a meeting place and a visible symbol of resistance to British attempts to tax them. It towered above the rooftops of the city and was located just outside the Upper Barracks, where many British troops were garrisoned. It sent those troops a clear message: the colonists were prepared to fight for their liberty.

The Boston Massacre (1770)

After the repeal of the Stamp Act, the colonists celebrated and the British tried to think up new ways of raising money. Their solution was the Revenue Act of 1767, which returned to the tried and tested method of raising money through customs duties (see table on page 69). The colonists immediately began to carry out peaceful measures to resist the new Act, such as a boycott, but events took a violent turn in Boston.

The significance of Boston

Boston was the city most affected by the Revenue Act because the headquarters of the new American Board of Customs Commissioners was set up there to regulate trade with the colonies. This was an unpopular move and mobs began to attack customs officials as soon as they arrived in Boston. As a result, the British placed troops in the city to control the locals. By 1769, there were

4,000 British soldiers in Boston, which had a population of around 15,500. In such a crowded place, the distrust between the troops and colonists intensified.

Source A

Mercy Warren, a colonist in Boston, witnessed the arrival of the first troops in the city. She recalled the event in a book called *History of the Rise, Progress and Termination of the American Revolution* (1805).

The American war may be dated from the hostile parade of this day; a day which marks with... [shame] the councils of Britain. At this period the inhabitants of the colonies almost universally breathed an unshaken loyalty to the King of England, and the strongest attachment to a country whence they derived their origin. Thus was the astonishment of the whole province excited, when to the grief and consternation of the town of Boston several regiments were landed, and marched sword in hand through the principal streets of their city, then in... peace.

The events of March 1770

On 5 March 1770, a crowd of around 100 gathered outside the Customs House. They threw snowballs, icicles and oyster shells at the British guards. One soldier, Private Hugh Montgomery, fell to the ground. When he got up, he fired his musket. In response, around five other soldiers thought the order had been given to fire. They each fired off one or two shots into the crowd at point blank range, killing four colonists immediately; one died later and eight were wounded. This became known as the Boston Massacre.

Impact of the Boston Massacre

The Boston Massacre was a flashpoint in the relationship between the British authorities and the American colonists. For the British, it was a clear sign that they needed to back off, or face another confrontation with the colonists. They chose to calm the situation and their troops were led out of the city to Castle William in Boston Harbor. For the colonists, the massacre had two important consequences.

- **It created propaganda for the anti-British cause:** Paul Revere, a member of the Boston Sons of Liberty and a political cartoonist, produced an engraving of the Boston Massacre (see Source B) that was widely publicised. It helped turn the colonists against the British.

- **A committee of correspondence was set up:** in order to resist future British measures, in September 1771, Boston set up a committee to strengthen links within the colony and to the other colonies.

Activity ?

Get into groups of three.

- **a** One person should use Source B to argue that the British are bullies.

- **b** The second person should argue that Source B inaccurately represents British treatment of the colonists.

- **c** The third person should listen, then decide and explain which was the most convincing argument.

British and American relations: the Boston Tea Party, 1773

By 1770, thanks to the combined efforts of the colonists, most of the terms of the Revenue Act had been repealed. Only one, the duty on tea, still remained in force. In 1773, the British attempt to increase the amount collected on this duty once again led to unintended consequences.

Source B

A coloured engraving entitled *The Bloody Massacre on 5th March, 1770*, by Paul Revere. It was produced immediately after the Boston Massacre and was circulated widely.

The Tea Act (1773)

The Tea Act was passed by Parliament in 1773. It was designed to help the East India Company sell its tea by making it cheaper. The company no longer had to pay the 12 pence per pound tax charged on the tea as it passed through Britain. Instead, it only paid the 3 pence tax charged under the Revenue Act of 1767. The Act also helped the company to get customers, because only agents of the East India Company could sell the tea.

At face value, this looked like a good deal for the colonists because the price of tea would drop dramatically. However, the remaining duty of 3 pence per pound was viewed as yet another attempt to enforce British taxation on the colonists. The Tea Act also angered leading colonists, such as influential merchants and wealthy smugglers. Legal traders faced ruin because the East India Company now had monopoly control of the trade, while smugglers, who did not benefit from the refund, had to charge higher prices than the company agents.

They quickly united in their opposition to the tax and, on 5 November 1773, the members of a Boston town meeting* agreed to help them resist it.

> **Key term**
>
> **Town meeting***
>
> A formal and regular meeting of elected representatives in a town. It was a common structure for local government in New England.

The Boston Tea Party

The first tea ship, the *Dartmouth*, arrived in Boston Harbor on 28 November 1773, with two more following shortly after. In response, the Boston Committee of Correspondence began to guard the harbour to stop the tea from being unloaded. They wanted the ship to leave, but the governor, Thomas Hutchinson, was determined to wait until he could legally seize the tea. Customs officials could do this after a period of 20 days, if the duty on the tea had not been paid.

Events came to a head on 16 December 1773, a day before the governor could use force to confiscate and sell off the tea. About 5,000 people gathered in Boston's Old South Church and decided on a plan of action. Around 60 men, disguised as Native Americans, would break into the three ships and throw the tea into the water. When night fell, they carried out the plan and threw 342 chests of tea into the sea.

Consequences

The British authorities were horrified. The Bostonians had ruined £10,000 worth of tea, equivalent to over £1 million today, with no regard for the good intentions of the Tea Act. British authority had been challenged and the governor of Massachusetts had fled to his country house. Elsewhere in British America, tea ships were forced to return home before they landed. In some places, such as New York in March 1774, more tea was ruined. The relationship between Britain and the American colonies had begun to fall apart.

British and American relations: the Intolerable Acts

In March 1774, the British decided to punish the colonists of Boston for their actions during the Tea Party. They passed a series of Coercive Acts*, which the colonists called the Intolerable Acts. The table on page 75 provides a summary of their terms.

> **Key term**
>
> **Coercive (Intolerable) Acts***
>
> Acts that used force and restrictive measures to control Boston. They were introduced in Boston in 1774 as a punishment for the Boston Tea Party.

1. The first ship, the *Dartmouth*, arrived on 28 November 1773.

2. Two other tea ships arrived after the *Dartmouth*.

3. The Bostonians guarded Boston Harbor until 16 December 1773.

4. On 16 December 1773, 60 men headed to Boston Harbor.

5. Disguised as Native Americans, they threw the tea into the water.

6. The 342 chests of tea were worth £10,000.

Figure 3.3 The events of the Boston Tea Party.

Act	Key terms
Boston Port Act of 1774	• Boston's port would be closed to all traffic from 1 June 1774. • It would only be reopened when compensation had been paid to the East India Company.
Massachusetts Government Act of 1774	• The elected council in Massachusetts was replaced by one chosen by the British government. • More power was given to the governor of Massachusetts. • The number of town meetings in Massachusetts was reduced to one per year.
Impartial Administration of Justice Act of 1774	• Anyone who was accused of a capital crime* while stopping a riot would not be tried in the colony where they were accused. • The person would be tried in another colony or in England.
Quartering Act of 1774	• It renewed the terms of the Quartering Act of 1765 (see page 69). • Troops could now be housed with private families.

Key term

Capital crime*

A crime for which the death penalty can be given as a punishment.

Extend your knowledge

The Quebec Act of 1774

The Quebec Act, passed in June 1774, was not one of the Intolerable Acts. However, the colonists saw it as one. It set up the government of Quebec with a royal governor and a council, which were both appointed by the British government rather than elected. The Act also extended Quebec's territory to cover the Ohio Country (see Figure 2.4).

Why do you think the colonists saw the Quebec Act as part of the Intolerable Acts?

Significance of the Intolerable Acts

The Acts affected all Bostonians, not just those who had taken part in the Tea Party. For example, the Boston Port Act stopped supplies from reaching Boston, which made it more difficult to buy everyday necessities. In addition, the Quartering Act meant that soldiers could leave overcrowded barracks and stay in people's homes. As well as restricting everyday life, the Acts made it more difficult to riot because the Impartial Administration of Justice Act protected those who maintained British control. The effect was to turn even more people against the British, especially in Boston.

In response to the Intolerable Acts, the Bostonians tried to enforce a boycott of British goods, across all the colonies, called the Solemn League and Covenant. Although the Bostonians struggled to get support from the other colonies for the boycott, the Intolerable Acts did help to unite the colonists against Britain in two other ways.

• **The other colonies showed their support for Boston:** they sent food and supplies during the blockade of 1774.

• **The colonies decided to hold a Continental Congress:** this was a meeting, with elected delegates from most of the colonies, to decide on their response to the Intolerable Acts.

Exam-style question, Section A

Write a narrative account analysing the key events of 1770–74 that led to the Intolerable Acts (1774).

You may use the following in your answer:

• the Boston Massacre (1770)

• the Boston Tea Party (1773).

You **must** also use information of your own.   **8 marks**

Exam tip

This question targets your ability to write an analytical narrative. Try to find an event from the middle of the time frame of the question that links to the Boston Tea Party.

The significance of the First Continental Congress, 1774

Following the introduction of the Intolerable Acts, the colonists decided to co-ordinate their actions to get the Acts repealed. This was a significant decision because the colonists were now going to work together against Britain. Between 5 September 1774 and 26 October 1774, the First Continental Congress was held in Philadelphia. Fifty-five delegates from every colony except Georgia attended the meeting. They reached three major agreements.

1 **The Declaration of Colonial Rights and Grievances:** this document set out what the colonists believed were their rights. They argued that parliament could only control trade to benefit the whole empire, not use it to tax them.

2 **The Continental Association:** an agreement that the colonies would stop British imports and end the consumption of British goods. It went further than the Solemn League and Covenant because it would also stop exports to Britain.

3 **To set up committees of observation and inspection:** these were locally elected committees that would make sure the Continental Association agreement was obeyed.

Consequences of the First Continental Congress

Colonial governments began to shut down, as the colonists refused to pay taxes to them or follow their orders. Instead, the committees of observation and inspection (which at their height had around 7,000 members) or newly elected provincial congresses* took control of government in the colonies. They enforced the Continental Association through threats and intimidation, and they began to organise local militias called minutemen*. The colonies now had two governments, which competed for control.

Key terms

Provincial congress*

A form of colonial government with elected members. In Massachusetts, this was the name for the old colonial assembly, which continued to govern after 1774 without British support.

Minuteman*

Member of a militia who would turn up at short notice if an emergency occurred. Minutemen were loyal to the colonists rather than the British authorities.

This rivalry erupted into violence in April 1775. The colonists of Massachusetts had begun to arm themselves at a town called Concord, so the new British military governor, General Thomas Gage, decided to take action. On 18 April, he sent his troops to Concord, via Lexington, to arrest the leaders of the provincial congress and take their ammunition. The colonists resisted and, in the fighting that followed, 73 British troops and 49 colonists were killed. The first shots had been fired between the two sides and they were now at war.

The significance of the Second Continental Congress, 1775

After the fighting at Lexington and Concord, the first session of the Second Continental Congress met on 10 May 1775 until 2 August 1775. It now had representatives from every colony and had begun to act as a national government. Figure 3.4 shows the main decisions the Second Continental Congress took to oppose Britain.

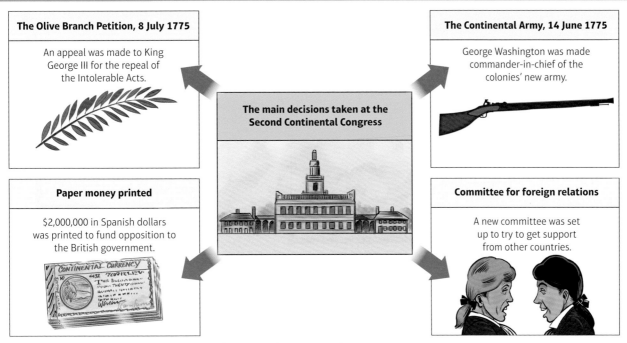

Figure 3.4 The main decisions made at the Second Continental Congress in 1775.

The decisions taken at the Second Continental Congress showed how far the conflict between Britain and the colonies had escalated due to the fighting at Lexington and Concord. In 1774, the First Continental Congress had organised peaceful measures to resist the British whereas, in 1775, the Second made preparations for war.

Up until this point the colonists, although in conflict with parliament, still showed loyalty to the king through the Olive Branch Petition (see Figure 3.4). All this changed on 23 August 1775 when George III rejected the petition and declared that the 13 colonies were in a state of rebellion. Parliament confirmed this on 22 December 1775 when they passed the American Prohibitory Act. The Act banned trade with British America and stated that the Royal Navy could seize American ships. As far as Britain was concerned, the colonists were now rebels rather than protestors.

Division in the colonies

The Second Continental Congress left the colonists with three choices. They could join the rebels and the fight against Britain, they could remain neutral or they could become loyalists*. Around 40% decided to remain neutral and a further 20% actively supported the British.

These divisions meant that the war that raged across the colonies until 1783 was not simply between the British and the colonists, but also between the colonists themselves.

Interpretation 1

An extract from the book *Revolutionary America 1763–1815* by Francis Cogliano, published in 2009. It explores the significance of the Second Continental Congress.

When the Second Continental Congress ended its first session on August 2, its members had accomplished much. They had organized the rebel war effort while attempting to stay within their stated defensive aims, and they had appealed directly to the king… That they prepared for war before adopting their appeal to the monarch indicates that most congressmen were not optimistic about the fate of their petition… If George III and his ministers would only listen to American appeals, then peace could be restored. Events over the next few months would prove to people on both sides of the Atlantic that reconciliation was impossible.

Key term

Loyalist*

A colonist who remained loyal to Britain in the War of Independence.

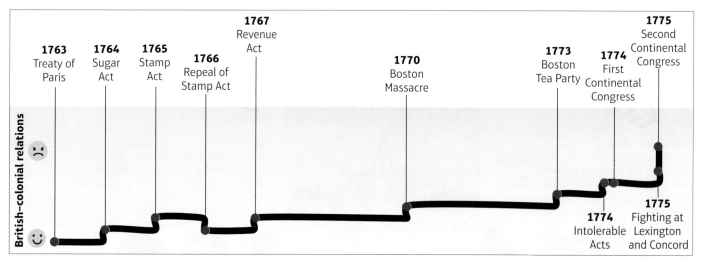

Figure 3.5 Increasing tensions between Britain and British America, 1763–75.

Summary

- British policies tried to raise money from the colonists through new taxes and duties.
- The colonists united against the Stamp Act (1765), led by the Sons of Liberty, to force its repeal.
- Events in Boston, including the Boston Massacre (1770) and the Boston Tea Party (1773), damaged relations between Britain and the colonists.
- Parliament punished the colonists for the Boston Tea Party with the Intolerable Acts (1774).

- The First Continental Congress (1774) organised a complete boycott of trade with Britain in response to the Intolerable Acts.
- The Second Continental Congress (1775) prepared the colonies for war with Britain and appointed George Washington the commander-in-chief of its new army.
- Britain declared that the colonies were in a state of rebellion and passed the American Prohibitory Act (1775).

Checkpoint

Strengthen

S1 Select and summarise the main ways the colonists resisted the Stamp Act.

S2 List and describe three events that damaged relations between Britain and the North American colonies between 1770 and 1775.

S3 Explain the main differences between the First Continental Congress (1774) and the Second Continental Congress (1775).

Challenge

C1 The significance of an event or development can be measured by its impact on people, their relationships and their reactions to it. Rank the following in terms of their significance:

- the Stamp Act (1765)
- the Boston Tea Party (1773)
- the Second Continental Congress (1775).

C2 What criteria did you use to make your decision?

C3 Choose another significant event or development in this section of the chapter. Explain, using your criteria, what made it significant.

How confident do you feel about your answers to these questions? If you're not sure you answered them well, draw up a table with two columns headed 'Events' and 'Consequences'. Fill out the table using notes from this section of the chapter.

3.2 The War of Independence, 1775–83

Learning outcomes

- Understand the significance of Thomas Paine's 'Common Sense' and Thomas Jefferson's work on the Declaration of Independence.
- Understand the events of the War of Independence, including key American victories at Saratoga and Yorktown.
- Understand the key factors that affected the course of the war, including the leadership of Washington, British mistakes and French and Spanish support for the Americans.
- Understand the significance of the Treaty of Paris, including Benjamin Franklin's contribution to the negotiations.

The influence of Thomas Paine's 'Common Sense'

'Common Sense' was a pamphlet written by Thomas Paine and published on 10 January 1776, after war had broken out. In it he made several arguments.

- **Against the British government:** he challenged the idea of monarchy, which limited the freedom of the British parliament.
- **In favour of independence:** he thought it would bring greater freedom in trade and politics. He also said that it would help Americans to gain support from other countries.
- **For a new republic*:** he wanted more people to have a say in their government, and an elected president to lead them.

His text was highly influential, because his writing style was designed to appeal to a wider audience than previous political pamphlets. He wrote using everyday language and illustrated his arguments with familiar references from the Bible. This style helped him to sell 100,000 copies of 'Common Sense', which went through 25 editions in its first year. As a result, he changed the views of Americans. Instead of a desire for reform or the repeal of British laws, they now wanted independence.

Key term

Republic*

A government where the people vote for their representatives to run the country on their behalf. A republic usually has a president as its head of state, rather than a monarch or emperor.

Source A

An excerpt from Thomas Paine's 'Common Sense', published in 1776. It is a criticism of the origins of the British monarchy.

England, since the conquest, hath known some few good monarchs, but groaned beneath a much larger number of bad ones; yet no man in his senses can say that their claim under William the Conqueror is a very honourable one. A French bastard, landing with an armed banditti [gang] and establishing himself king of England against the consent of the natives, is in plain terms a very... [poor] original.

The significance of the Declaration of Independence

From April 1776 onwards, the colonies began to give their representatives in Congress* permission to vote for independence. In response to this, Congress created a Declaration Committee, which comprised Thomas Jefferson, Benjamin Franklin and three other men to write a Declaration of Independence. After Congress made several changes to the Committee's draft, it was adopted on 4 July 1776.

Key term

Congress*

A governing body made up of elected representatives. The Second Continental Congress became known as Congress once the War of Independence (1775–83) had begun.

Source B

An early 19th-century painting by John Trumbull. It shows the Declaration Committee in the foreground. They are presenting the Declaration of Independence to Congress.

The role of Thomas Jefferson

Thomas Jefferson was a key member of the Declaration Committee that was formed on 10 June 1776. His role was to write the draft of the Declaration, which would then be reviewed by the committee and by Congress. After two weeks of intense activity, Jefferson had produced the text (see Source D) that would make him famous and become a symbol for the American Revolution. It had three main parts:

1 **An introduction:** this set out the ideas that inspired the document. It argued that all men are born with natural rights, which the government should protect.

2 **A list of King George III's crimes:** it listed 18 crimes committed by George III. These included closing down the colonists' assemblies, limiting their westward expansion and taxing them without their agreement.

3 **A conclusion:** the British government had not protected their natural rights, which meant the United States of America should be free and independent.

Significance

Once Congress had adopted the Declaration, it gave Americans independence as a goal to fight for. It also provided them with a long list of reasons why they should fight against the British. It was significantly different to earlier documents because:

- it was the first formal document to use the words 'United States of America'
- colonists' arguments were based on the idea that they had natural rights.

These two features increased the power of the argument against Britain. However, there were limits to the freedom the Declaration offered. It did not include natural rights for slaves or Native Americans, which meant that in the longer term an American victory would not benefit these groups.

Source C

An excerpt from the final version of the Declaration of Independence, which was adopted by Congress on 4 July 1776.

He [the King] has combined with others [parliament] to subject us to a… [control] foreign to our constitution… giving his assent to their acts of pretended legislation:

For quartering large bodies of armed troops among us;
…

For protecting them, by a mock trial, from punishment for any murders which they should commit on the inhabitants of these states;

For cutting off our trade with all parts of the world;

For imposing taxes on us without our consent;

Activity ?

Get into small groups. Each person should take one of the crimes listed in the Declaration of Independence (Source C) and find an example of it in this chapter. Share your findings with one another.

Source D

An excerpt from the introduction of the Declaration of Independence, which has become the most well-known part of the document.

We hold these truths to be self-evident: That all men are created equal; that they are endowed by their Creator with certain unalienable rights; that among these are life, liberty, and the pursuit of happiness; that, to secure these rights, governments are instituted among men, deriving their just powers from the consent of the governed; that whenever any form of government becomes destructive of these ends, it is the right of the people to alter or to abolish it, and to institute new government, laying its foundation on such principles, and organizing its powers in such form, as to them shall seem most likely to effect their safety and happiness.

The course of the war

The War of Independence had begun in 1775, when the first fighting between the British and Americans occurred at Lexington and Concord. Initially, the British focused their war effort in the northern colonies and secured control of New York City and Philadelphia. However, after a humiliating surrender to the Americans at Saratoga in 1777, the British turned to the south. They took Charleston, but struggled to keep control of the areas they captured. Small-scale battles continued until the British, awaiting fresh troops for their southern campaign, were defeated at Yorktown in 1781. After this, they began to seek peace with the Americans. The key battles are described in the table on page 82 and shown in Figure 3.6.

Exam-style question, Section A

Explain **two** of the following:

- The importance of the First Continental Congress (1774) for relations between Britain and British America
- The importance of Thomas Paine's 'Common Sense' (1776) for the American colonists' attitude to Britain
- The importance of the Declaration of Independence (1776) for the development of the War of Independence.

16 marks

Exam tip

This question targets your ability to explain the importance of an event or development. Use specific detail from the event or development to support your explanation.

Source E

An early 19th-century painting of General Burgoyne's surrender at Saratoga to General Horatio Gates, by John Trumbull. It was the first major British defeat in the war.

Stage	Key battle or siege	Outcomes	Significance
The beginning of the war	Battle of Bunker Hill (Massachusetts, June 1775)	• British suffer heavy losses. • British secure control of Boston. • American army withdraws but remains intact.	British victory but they abandon Boston in 1776.
	Battle of Long Island (New York, August 1776)	• After the battle, Washington was driven out of New York City. • 300 Americans killed and 1,100 wounded or captured. • Washington's army escapes and wins small victories against British.	British secure control of New York City, which was used as the British army headquarters.
The northern campaign	Battle of Brandywine Creek (Pennsylvania, September 1777)	• Washington fails to stop British march on Philadelphia. • Americans attack British again at Germantown, but fail. • American army survives battle, but loses Philadelphia.	British victory, but they abandon Philadelphia in 1778.
	Battle of Bemis Heights and surrender at Saratoga (New York, Oct 1777)	• British forces defeated. • 5,800 British surrender at Saratoga.	American victory that led to greater French involvement in the war.
The southern campaign	Siege of Charleston (South Carolina, February to May 1780)	• British capture Charleston. • 2,571 Americans surrender. • Americans lose huge amount of weapons and supplies.	British victory that helped secure control of the southern colonies.
	Siege of Yorktown (Virginia, October 1781)	• British surrender to Washington. • 299 British killed and 8,000 prisoners taken.	American victory that encouraged the British to make peace.

Key American victories: Saratoga, 1777

The plan

In 1777, a British general, John Burgoyne, planned a campaign to conquer New England. His idea was to send two forces, including British soldiers, Hessian* troops and Native Americans, southwards from Canada, under two leaders. Burgoyne would march down the Hudson River valley to the British base in New York, while Lieutenant Colonel Barry St Leger would take the rest of the troops down the St Lawrence River to meet him. He hoped this show of force would divide the colonies and bring the rebellion to an end.

Events of 1777

On 20 June 1777, 8,300 troops left Montreal and soon ran into difficulties. Burgoyne's force struggled to travel more than a mile a day through forests, whilst St Leger was defeated by the Americans at Oriskany and forced to retreat.

Key term

Hessian*

A German soldier. The British hired 29,166 German troops, many of them from the state of Hesse–Kassel, to fight alongside them in North America.

By September, Burgoyne had made little progress, and the Americans led by Horatio Gates blocked his path. He tried to clear the way at the Battle of Bemis Heights (see table on page 82), but he could not defeat the Americans. On 17 October 1777, his 5,800 troops surrendered at Saratoga and were sent to Virginia until the end of the war.

Consequences

The 1777 campaign had been a disaster for the British. It had a number of significant consequences.

- **The British appealed for peace:** the prime minister, Lord North, offered the Americans a return to the way things had been in 1763. The Americans refused.
- **The British commander-in-chief resigned:** General William Howe stepped down from the role of commander-in-chief of the British forces in North America and was replaced by Sir Henry Clinton.
- **The French became involved in the war:** after Saratoga, the French realised the Americans had a chance of success. They signed two treaties to support the American war effort (see page 87).

Exam-style question, Section A

Explain **two** consequences of the British surrender at Saratoga (1777). **8 marks**

Exam tip

This question is asking you about consequence. It is regarding a battle so you should consider the consequences for both sides in the conflict.

Key American victories: Yorktown, 1781

General Charles Cornwallis was the leader of the British campaign to take control of the southern colonies. He achieved considerable success (see table on page 82), but in the process had exhausted his army. In order to rest and resupply his 7,200 troops, he took them to Yorktown in August 1781 and set up a naval base there. He then waited for supplies to arrive from New York City.

However, the French Admiral de Grasse arrived with 20 ships and blocked access to Yorktown. Unable to resupply and separated from Clinton's forces in New York, Cornwallis was extremely vulnerable. However, he took little action and waited for help that never reached him. On 28 September 1781, 17,000 American and French soldiers, led by Washington and the French Comte de Rochambeau, began a combined attack on Yorktown.

Impact of the siege of Yorktown

On 19 October 1781, worn down by the siege of Yorktown, Cornwallis surrendered. When the news was received in Britain, enthusiasm for the war disappeared. After some debate, on 27 February 1782 parliament voted to end the war in America and to negotiate peace terms. The major campaigns of the War of Independence were now at an end.

Interpretation 1

An extract from the book *America: Empire of Liberty* by David Reynolds, published in 2009. It explores the significance of the defeat at Yorktown.

Saratoga turned the war; Yorktown decided it. Without American courage and stamina, the struggle could easily have been lost, yet without French support, outright victory would have been difficult to attain. The conflict could have dragged on for years, with the British controlling some parts of the seaboard and the Americans others. But after Yorktown, Americans knew that a victorious peace was only a matter of time. After a lengthy diplomatic finale, in September 1783 the British signed the Treaty of Paris, acknowledging full independence for the United States.

Significant factors

Three main factors affected the course of the American War of Independence. These were:

- the contributions of General George Washington to the American war effort
- British mistakes and the weaknesses in their plans for the war
- support from the French and Spanish for the American rebels.

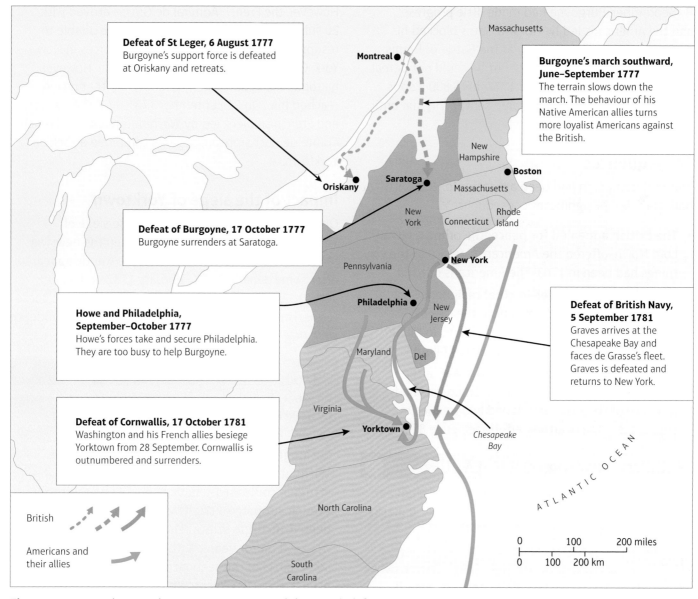

Defeat of St Leger, 6 August 1777
Burgoyne's support force is defeated at Oriskany and retreats.

Burgoyne's march southward, June–September 1777
The terrain slows down the march. The behaviour of his Native American allies turns more loyalist Americans against the British.

Defeat of Burgoyne, 17 October 1777
Burgoyne surrenders at Saratoga.

Howe and Philadelphia, September–October 1777
Howe's forces take and secure Philadelphia. They are too busy to help Burgoyne.

Defeat of British Navy, 5 September 1781
Graves arrives at the Chesapeake Bay and faces de Grasse's fleet. Graves is defeated and returns to New York.

Defeat of Cornwallis, 17 October 1781
Washington and his French allies besiege Yorktown from 28 September. Cornwallis is outnumbered and surrenders.

British

Americans and their allies

Figure 3.6 A map showing the major campaigns and the British defeats at Saratoga and Yorktown.

The significance of Washington's role

Contribution 1: keeping the army together

General George Washington was the commander-in-chief of the Continental Army from July 1775 until the end of the war. One of his most important contributions to the war effort was his ability to stop the army from falling apart or being completely defeated by the British. There are several examples of how he did this.

- **Strategic retreats:** at the Battle of Long Island, he organised a retreat on 29 August 1776, which stopped the main body of his army from being captured.

- **Looking after his troops:** when his army had to spend the winter at Morristown, New Jersey, in early 1777, he arranged for smallpox inoculations to be given to his soldiers.

- **Maintaining discipline:** he established a strict disciplinary code in the army, which encouraged soldiers to respect and obey their officers.

Extend your knowledge

The winter at Valley Forge, 1777–78

In late 1777, Washington marched 11,000 troops into their winter camp at Valley Forge, near Philadelphia. The conditions were dreadful, with little food and freezing temperatures. In order to keep the army together, Washington organised foraging parties to gather supplies, but also issued passes to limit the numbers who could leave the camp. Despite these measures, 2,500 died and 1,000 deserted.

Look back at the table on page 82. What connection can you find between the events of 1777 and the numbers who wanted to desert at Valley Forge?

Contribution 2: taking opportunities

Washington did not follow the traditional habits of European warfare. Instead, he took any opportunity that presented itself. For example, European wars were not usually fought in winter. However, Washington defeated British forces at Trenton in December 1776 and Princeton in January 1777 because they were not prepared for his attacks.

He also made effective use of any advantage that presented itself. For instance, when an experienced Prussian officer offered to train American troops in February 1778, even though he spoke no English, Washington accepted. It turned out to be a good decision because the officer, Baron von Steuben, helped to train the Continental Army to march in order and to use its weapons more effectively.

Contribution 3: encouraging support

Washington was able to muster* huge numbers of colonists to fight for him. He promoted the idea of the 'glorious cause' of American liberty, which convinced people to join the army. He also respected civilians.

Key term

Muster*

To raise troops. During the war, the rebels relied on local militias to fight alongside the Continental Army. The British also appealed to loyal colonists to fight on their behalf.

When his army needed supplies, he paid for them or gave receipts for seized property. As a result, more supported the rebel cause. Around 230,000 men served in the Continental Army throughout the war.

He also gained the support of key figures that could help the Americans win victory. When the British were trapped at Yorktown in 1781, French Admiral de Grasse wanted to take his ships from the Chesapeake Bay where they were preventing supplies from reaching the British. It was Washington who persuaded him to stay until the siege could begin. Another important officer, the Marquis de Lafayette, who also played a central role in the siege of Yorktown, was encouraged by Washington to join his staff before the French had even become involved in the war.

Overall, it was due to this ability to preserve the army, together with his inspirational qualities and his willingness to take advantage of opportunities, that the Americans eventually achieved success in the war.

Source F

A painting of George Washington and his generals at Yorktown in 1781, painted in the 1780s by Charles Willson Peale, who was an officer during the war.

British mistakes

Mistake 1: poor battle plans

Bad planning played an important role in the British failure to defeat the Americans. There were several consequences of their poor planning.

- **Victories with heavy casualties:** at Bunker Hill (1775), which involved a frontal assault on the Americans, 228 British soldiers were killed and 800 wounded.
- **Many Americans escaped capture:** after the Battle of Long Island (1776), the British did not follow up their victory, which meant 9,000 American troops escaped to fight again.
- **Huge logistical* problems:** during the 1777 campaign, General Burgoyne took 30 carts full of possessions with him. This slowed his army down and contributed to its surrender at Saratoga.

> ### Key term
>
> **Logistics***
>
> The organisation of troop movements and their housing and supplies.

Mistake 2: poor communication

The British generals struggled to work together. In 1777, General Howe planned a campaign to capture Philadelphia, but did not co-ordinate this with Burgoyne's plan to march south to New York. As a consequence, Howe was too busy at Philadelphia to help Burgoyne when he ran into difficulties on his journey through New York.

The same problem continued throughout the war. In 1781, General Clinton sent Cornwallis to Yorktown. When the Americans began to surround Yorktown, Clinton sent a letter that promised reinforcements of 4,000 British troops. However, he did not live up to this promise. Instead, Clinton delayed and Cornwallis waited for help that never came. By mid-October, an outnumbered Cornwallis surrendered to Washington.

Mistake 3: poor behaviour

The British did little to maintain the support of American loyalists or gain the support of neutral Americans. In fact, the behaviour of their troops turned many against the British. This was because the British relied on hired Hessian troops and Native American allies, who frightened Americans with their violent behaviour. In response, many Americans joined the rebels.

> ### Source G
>
> An early 19th-century painting of the Battle of Bunker Hill (1775) by John Trumbull. It shows the frontal assault the British used in an attempt to take the rebels' strong defensive position.

French and Spanish involvement in the war

Figure 3.7 below demonstrates the huge impact that French and Spanish involvement had on the War of Independence. The main consequence of their joint involvement was that it became a worldwide war. The French had 64 warships and the Spanish had 57, which outnumbered the 90 Britain possessed. Britain had to protect itself and its other colonies from an invasion so British troops and ships were moved around. In 1778, 41% of Britain's navy was in America, but this had dropped to 13% by 1780.

Spanish involvement meant that Britain had to send troops to protect East and West Florida from an invasion, but the most active support for the war came from the French, who provided the Americans with:

- **vital supplies:** the French sent around £48 million worth of weapons and supplies during the war
- **military expertise:** French officers took a central role in planning campaigns. For example, the Marquis de Lafayette joined Washington's staff in July 1777
- **a fleet of ships:** Admiral de Grasse's French fleet helped prevent supplies reaching Yorktown and ferried French troops to join the siege itself.

February 1778
The French sign a trade agreement and a Treaty of Alliance with the Americans.

March 1778
The British decide to focus on the southern colonies and the protection of the West Indies

June 1778
The British abandon Philadelphia, as the French fleet may blockade it.

May 1779
Spain joins with France to try and regain Gibraltar. The British move troops to Florida in case the Spanish try to retake it.

February 1780
The French order the comte de Rochambeau, with 6,000 troops, to North America.

August 1781
Admiral de Grasse's French fleet reaches Yorktown. This helps Washington to stop the resupply of the British base.

Figure 3.7 French and Spanish involvement in the war, 1778–81.

Activities ?

Work in groups of five. Give one person the role of the British prime minister. The rest should choose from: a British general, an American general, the French foreign minister and a loyalist.

1 On a big sheet of paper, the prime minister should write a short post for a social networking site announcing the news of the first event in the table on page 82. The rest of the group should in turn write their comments underneath.

2 Repeat with each event in the table.

3 Based on your group's comments, decide what the most significant event in the war was. Share your decision with the class.

The Treaty of Paris, 1783

Peace negotiations

On 15 April 1782, a British negotiator arrived in France. His job was to open up direct talks with the Americans, without French involvement. He met with three Americans who had been chosen by Congress to represent them in peace talks. This group, which included Benjamin Franklin, had been told to work alongside the French to negotiate a peace treaty. However, they ignored these instructions, out of fear that the French would want to give too much American territory away to their Spanish ally, and agreed a draft treaty with Britain on 29 November 1782. After much diplomatic effort, the French agreed to the terms on 23 September 1783 and the war formally ended.

The role of Benjamin Franklin

Franklin was the American representative of the middle states. He played a central role in the peace negotiations.

- **He established America's main demands**: on 10 July 1782 he set out the terms the British must agree to. It included recognition of American independence and the boundaries of the United States, the removal of British troops from the 13 colonies and an agreement on fishing rights off Newfoundland.

- **He maintained good relations with the French:** the French foreign minister, Vergennes, was furious that the Americans had negotiated with the British in secret. Franklin helped to repair American–French relations and secure their continued support.

Although Franklin's contributions were vital to the success of the Treaty of Paris, there were limits to his achievements. In August and September 1782, when many of the talks between Britain and America took place, Franklin was too ill to join in. In addition, although Franklin's main demands were met in the Treaty of Paris, his additional ones, such as giving Canada to the United States, were not. The treaty that was signed in 1783 owed much to Franklin, but not everything.

Exam-style question, Section A

Write a narrative account analysing the key events of 1778–83 that led to the Treaty of Paris (1783).

You may use the following in your answer:
- the French sign the Treaty of Alliance (1778)
- the British surrender at Yorktown (1781).

You **must** also use information of your own.   **8 marks**

Exam tip

This question targets your ability to write an analytical narrative. A strong answer will use events from across the whole time frame of the question.

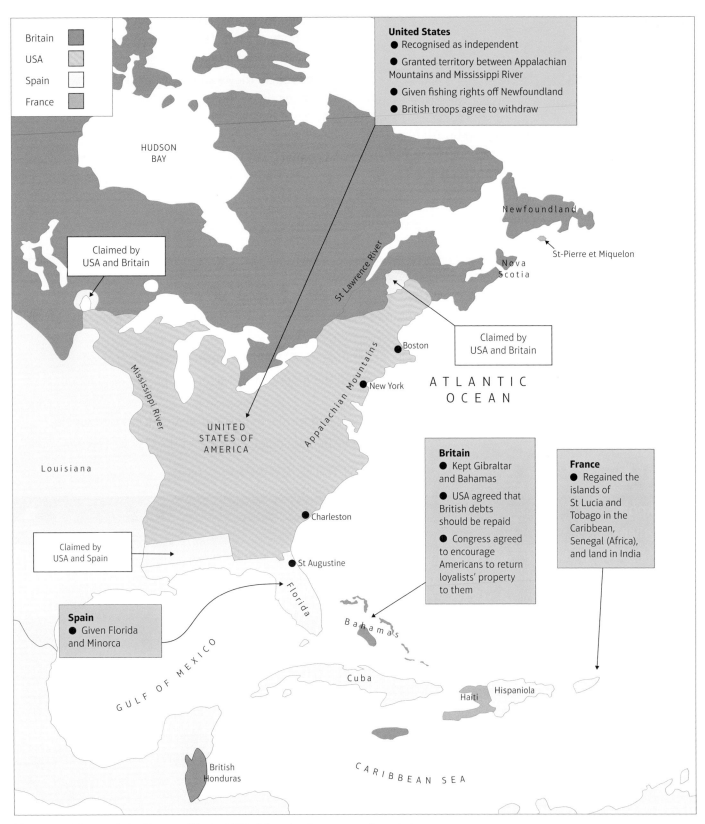

Figure 3.8 Terms of the Treaty of Paris, 1783. After the Treaty was signed, there were some disputes about the areas defined by its terms.

The treaty

The Treaty of Paris was good news for the citizens of the United States of America (USA), which was now recognised as an independent country. The terms (see Figure 3.8) were extremely generous to the USA because Britain wanted to establish a strong trading partnership with it. Once the treaty was in force, the British began to evacuate. By 4 December 1783, most of the British troops had left. However, there were several groups who did not benefit from the treaty.

- **Native Americans:** they were not mentioned in the Treaty of Paris. Their land was now at risk from aggressive US expansion.
- **The French:** they wanted a weak USA that would have to rely on them. The amount of land the USA received in the treaty meant it had little to fear from the French.
- **Loyalists:** the treaty gave little protection to loyalists and did not create a way to enforce the return of their confiscated property. Many left the USA as a result (see page 94).

Summary

- Thomas Paine's 'Common Sense' (1776) encouraged Americans to seek independence.
- The Declaration of Independence (1776) was drafted by Thomas Jefferson and gave Americans a clear goal to fight for.
- The Americans forced British armies to surrender at Saratoga (1777) and Yorktown (1781).
- George Washington, with French and Spanish support, led the Americans to victory in the War of Independence (1775–83).
- British generals followed bad plans, communicated poorly and turned many neutral Americans into rebels.
- The Treaty of Paris (1783), which was largely negotiated by Benjamin Franklin, meant the USA was recognised as an independent country.

Checkpoint

Strengthen

S1 What examples can you find of Americans showing they wanted independence?

S2 Select and summarise the main events in the War of Independence (1775–83).

S3 What facts or ideas show that the Americans were successful in the War of Independence?

Challenge

C1 Explain one shared consequence of the publication of 'Common Sense' (1776) and the Declaration of Independence (1776).

C2 How is the surrender at Yorktown (1781) related to the surrender at Saratoga (1777)?

C3 How would you prove that the Treaty of Paris (1783) was important for a range of groups?

How confident do you feel about your answers to these questions? If you're not sure you have answered them well, draw up a timeline of the events in this section of the chapter. Annotate each event with an effect it had.

The significance of the Declaration of Independence for slavery

The Declaration of Independence (1776) said that 'all men are created equal'. Thomas Jefferson's original draft also included a charge against King George III for encouraging the slave trade (see Source A). However, Congress removed this charge from the final draft, which meant the Declaration did not specifically mention slavery. It allowed each rebel colony to decide whether the clause applied to slaves or not.

Source A

An excerpt from Jefferson's original draft of the Declaration of Independence (1776). It was removed from the final version by Congress.

... he [George III] has waged cruel war against human nature itself, violating its most sacred rights of life & liberty in the persons of a distant people, who never offended him, captivating and carrying them into slavery in another hemisphere, or to incur miserable death in their transportation thither... [He was] determined to keep open a market where MEN should be bought & sold, he has... [stopped] every legislative attempt to prohibit or restrain this execrable commerce... he now is now exciting those very people to rise in arms among us, and to purchase that liberty of which he has deprived them...

The significance for slaves

Slaves in the northern colonies benefitted from the Declaration. In the constitution* of Massachusetts (1780) it stated that 'all men are born free and equal'. This clause, slaves claimed, meant that they were entitled to their freedom. As a result, from April 1781, a series of court cases took place in which slaves successfully sued for their freedom. These actions helped end slavery in Massachusetts.

Extend your knowledge

The Quok Walker case, 1781

A slave called Quok Walker took part in the first court case to free a slave in Massachusetts. In 1781, Walker ran away from his master, Nathaniel Jennison, to work for a neighbour. When Jennison tried to sue his neighbour, Walker countersued. Jennison lost the case because of the 'born free' clause in the constitution of Massachusetts, and Walker gained his freedom.

How strong is the link between the Quok Walker case and the Declaration of Independence?

In other rebel colonies, such as Pennsylvania in 1780, laws were passed to begin the abolition of slavery. Even in the south, where the economy was dependent on slaves, some progress was made. For example, in 1782, the Virginia Assembly said that owners could free their slaves in their last will and testament*. The Declaration had therefore started the process of abolition, but the results depended on local circumstances.

Key terms

Constitution*

A document that sets out how a state or nation is to be governed. After the colonies broke away from Britain, they had to establish the rules of their new national and state governments.

Last will and testament*

A legal document that says what will happen to a person's money and property after their death.

Limitations

Despite the good intentions of the Declaration, it did not bring about complete equality. The southern colonies relied on slaves, which meant that they:

- **limited who was classed as 'equal':** in the Virginia Declaration of Rights, for example, it was made clear that slaves were not a part of Virginian society and so did not have equal rights
- **did little to help slaves gain freedom:** therefore around 80,000 southern slaves escaped during the war because they knew independence would not mean freedom for them.

The picture in the northern and middle colonies was better, but outside of Massachusetts there were limits to the Declaration's impact on slavery. For example, in New York it took until 1799 for slavery to be abolished, which suggests the abolition movement there was only weakly linked to the Declaration. Slavery did gradually disappear from the north and become a southern institution, but the Declaration played only a small part in this long-term process.

The argument in Congress

The argument in the rebel colonies

The reaction of slaves

Figure 3.9 The significance of the Declaration of Independence for slavery.

Activities ?

1. Get into small groups. Each person should take on one of the roles from Figure 3.9, except that of Jefferson. Then:
   a. Pair up with one or two people whose opinion you agree with. Explain to the group why you agree.
   b. Look at your character's point in the diagram. Add some evidence to support the point and turn it into a short speech.
2. Draw up a table with each of the roles as column headings. Then:
   a. Take it in turns to present your short speech.
   b. In your table, record any facts or ideas each person uses.
3. Decide as a group who the Declaration of Independence had the greatest effect on.

The consequences of the war for the Native Americans

Many Native American tribes had sided with the British during the War of Independence and fought alongside them. However, when the British abandoned the war in 1783, the Treaty of Paris offered no protection for Native Americans. Instead, they were left to look after themselves. The first challenge they faced was to repair the damage that had been done by the war to their relationship with neighbouring nations and each other. The table below summarises the situation in 1783.

Relationship	Description
Native Americans and the USA	The USA saw most Native Americans as enemies. It made them accept blame for the war and sign treaties that gave up land, leaving them with only some reserved land to live on. For example, a treaty signed at Fort Stanwix (1784) took land from the Iroquois League*.
Native Americans and each other	Old alliances had broken up during the war, with some supporting the British and some the Americans. After the war, more divisions followed, as some chiefs signed treaties with the Americans, which their allied chiefs rejected.
Native Americans and European powers	The British would no longer provide military help. However, the British in Canada and the Spanish in Florida and the western half of the continent offered a place for Native Americans to escape to.

Key term

Iroquois League*

An alliance between several tribes. The Iroquois League represented six tribes in upper New York State, which broke up after the War of Independence.

Source B

An extract from a speech given by a delegation of 260 Native Americans from several tribes to the Spanish governor of Saint Louis in 1784.

The Americans, a great deal more ambitious and numerous than the English, put us out of our lands, forming therein great settlements, extending themselves like a plague of locusts in the territories of the Ohio River which we inhabit. They treat us as their cruellest enemies are treated, so that today hunger and the impetuous torrent of war which they impose upon us with other terrible calamities, have brought our villages to a struggle with death.

The frontier

The Treaty of Paris (1783) reignited the problems over land ownership that had caused the French and Indian War (1754–63), Pontiac's Rebellion (1763–66) and the actions of the Paxton Boys (1763–64). It surrendered control of areas like the Ohio Country to the USA, which resulted in trouble along its borders. Instead of a ceasefire, the fighting continued as Americans claimed more and more Native American land. In response, Native Americans raided frontier settlements, burned crops, stole horses and killed settlers and traders. The situation only began to calm after the USA negotiated treaties with Native Americans, or forced them to flee from their lands permanently.

The destination of Native Americans

Many Native Americans realised that without help from a rival foreign power, they stood little chance against the USA. As a result, they chose to leave their ancestral lands*. The map on page 94 indicates where they went.

Key term

Ancestral lands*

Lands which Native American tribes had lived on for many years.

Activities ?

Imagine it is 1783 and you are a Native American leader living in the Ohio Country.

1   Draw up a list of pros and cons for the following choices:

   a   negotiate with the Americans

   b   flee to Canada

   c   stay and fight.

2   Choose one option. Justify your decision.

3   Imagine you have met another leader who fought in the French and Indian War (1754–63). He remembers Pontiac's Rebellion (1763–66). What do you think he will advise? Explain your answer.

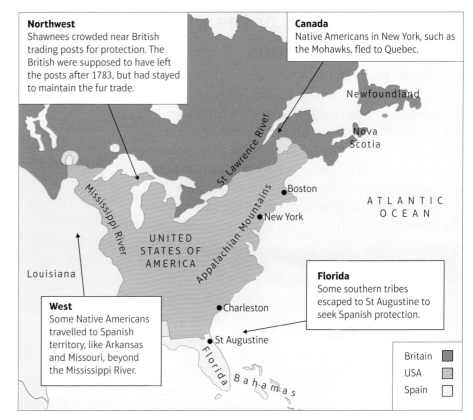

Northwest
Shawnees crowded near British trading posts for protection. The British were supposed to have left the posts after 1783, but had stayed to maintain the fur trade.

Canada
Native Americans in New York, such as the Mohawks, fled to Quebec.

West
Some Native Americans travelled to Spanish territory, like Arkansas and Missouri, beyond the Mississippi River.

Florida
Some southern tribes escaped to St Augustine to seek Spanish protection.

Britain ▪
USA ▪
Spain ▫

Figure 3.10 The destination of Native American refugees.

Exam-style question, Section A

Explain **two** consequences of the War of Independence (1775–83) for the Native Americans.

8 marks

Exam tip

This question is asking you about consequence. It specifies a group so you should focus your answer on them.

The impact of the war on loyalists

During the War of Independence, around 20% of the 2.5 million white colonists remained loyal to the British Empire. Many were prepared to stand up for their mother country and 19,000 signed up to fight against the American rebels. However, once the war was over, the defeated loyalists faced two main problems.

- **Threats and attacks from American mobs:** there were 42 loyalist units that fought in the war. They were very unpopular with the victorious rebels and were the targets of mob violence.

- **Their property was taken and sold by the rebels:** after the war, loyalists tried to claim over £10 million in compensation from the British. They received about £3 million.

As a consequence of these problems, many chose to go to other parts of the British Empire. In total, around 60,000 loyalists left their homes, taking around 15,000 slaves with them.

Black loyalists

On 7 November 1775, the governor of Virginia, the Earl of Dunmore, offered slaves their freedom if they agreed to fight for the British cause. For that reason, around 20,000 slaves joined the British during the War of Independence. Of this number, about 10,000 survived, received their freedom and were evacuated at the end of the war alongside white loyalists.

Loyalist resettlement in Nova Scotia and Quebec

In January 1783, loyalists began to make plans to leave the rebel colonies. They sent scouts to Port Roseway in Nova Scotia, and appealed to the governor of Halifax for help. Shortly after, in April, the first 7,000 loyalists began their journey from New York. By the end of the year, 30,000 had travelled to Nova Scotia and a further 5,000 to Quebec. Of those who went to Quebec, around 770 settled at Niagara. This had been an important British military post during the American Revolution and was also home to Native American refugees, who had settled there during the war.

Source C

A rare painting of a black loyalist woodcutter who had settled in Shelburne, Nova Scotia. This watercolour was done by artist William Booth in 1788.

The impact on their lives

It was a huge upheaval for loyalists to leave their homes behind and face an uncertain future, but their resettlement was made easier in several ways.

- **They were given land grants:** the governor of Halifax offered each white male settler a 300-acre plot. He arranged for 1.2 million acres in Nova Scotia to be distributed to the loyalists.
- **Loyalist towns quickly developed:** there were 8,000 settlers in the new loyalist town of Shelburne, Nova Scotia, by the end of 1783.
- **A new loyalist colony was established:** Quebec was split into Lower Canada, for established colonists, and Upper Canada, for loyalists, in 1791. Niagara became the first capital of Upper Canada.
- **Some black loyalists were given land:** free black people were offered land grants and, by early 1784, 1,485 black settlers had moved into Birchtown in Nova Scotia.

These measures helped to give the loyalists a fighting chance of success in their new lives, but their resettlement was not free of challenges. Some of the major problems the loyalists faced are shown in Figure 3.11 on page 96.

Source D

A letter written by Edward Winslow, who had been in charge of raising troops in Massachusetts, in 1784. It describes the treatment of former loyalist soldiers in Nova Scotia.

I saw all those Provincial Regiments (which we have so frequently mustered) landing in this inhospitable climate, in the month of October, without shelter and without knowing where to find a place to reside... Those respectable serjeants... were addressing me in a language which almost murdered me as I heard it.

'Sir, We have served all the War. Your honor is witness how faithfully! We were promised land, we expected you had obtained it for us, we like the country – only let us have a spot of our own, and give us such kind of regulations as will hinder bad men from reigning us.'

Winter	Integration	Black loyalists
Many struggled to survive their first winter in temporary housing or tents. Four hundred died in a single storm in Nova Scotia.	The loyalists and the older settlers did not get on. Nova Scotia was split up to create New Brunswick for the settlers in June 1784 and Quebec was split up in 1791.	Free black people received smaller land grants than white people. Slavery continued as 1,200 slaves also travelled with their masters to Nova Scotia.

Figure 3.11 The challenges that loyalists faced during resettlement.

Summary

- The Declaration of Independence (1776) helped many slaves in the northern states to gain their freedom.
- The Declaration did not help slaves in the south, which meant many decided to escape during the War of Independence (1775–83).
- Native American relations with the USA, as well as their relationship with other tribes, were damaged by the war.
- After the war, Americans increased their rate of settlement on Native American land, so many Native Americans were forced to leave their ancestral homes.
- Loyalists had their property taken from them during the war and faced violence and threats once it ended.
- Many loyalists chose to resettle in Nova Scotia and Quebec, but this was a difficult process.

Checkpoint

Strengthen

S1 Select two facts that prove the Declaration of Independence (1776) was significant for slaves and one that suggests it was not.

S2 Find and describe examples that show Native Americans suffered as a result of the War of Independence.

S3 Explain who the loyalists were and how their lives changed after the War of Independence.

Challenge

C1 When you are trying to judge how important an event or development is for a group of people, you should consider what stays the same as well as what it changes. Outline what stays the same for:

   a slaves in the southern states after the Declaration of Independence

   b Native Americans at the end of the War of Independence

   c black loyalists during their resettlement in Nova Scotia.

C2 Based on your answers to C1, discuss the idea that it would have been better for these groups if the Declaration of Independence and the war had never happened.

How confident are you about your answers? If you're unsure you answered them well, write a thought bubble for how slaves felt about the Declaration and how Native Americans and loyalists felt at the end of the war.

Recap: The loss of an empire, 1765–83

Recall quiz

Have a go at these 10 quick-fire questions:

1 What group was formed to resist the Stamp Act?

2 How many colonists were killed by the Boston Massacre?

3 Which event caused parliament to pass the Intolerable Acts in 1774?

4 At which Continental Congress was George Washington appointed commander-in-chief of the Continental Army?

5 Who drafted the Declaration of Independence?

6 Which country decided to help the USA after the British surrender at Saratoga?

7 Where did Cornwallis surrender to the Americans on 19 October 1781?

8 In what treaty did the British recognise the independence of the USA?

9 In which state did slaves use the courts to gain their freedom?

10 How many loyalists left the USA after the War of Independence: 15,000, 35,000 or 60,000?

Exam-style question, Section A

Explain **two** of the following:

- The importance of the Sons of Liberty for the failure of British attempts to tax the colonists
- The importance of the surrender at Yorktown (1781) for the American victory in the war
- The importance of the Declaration of Independence (1776) for slavery in the United States of America. **16 marks**

Exam tip

This question targets your ability to explain the importance of an event or development. Make sure you clearly explore how the situation from before the event or development was affected.

Activities

1 Copy and complete the table below:

In 1765	In 1783
The North American colonies were a part of the…	The United States of America was now…
Relations between the colonists and the British had begun to worsen because…	Relations between the USA and Britain had been severely damaged by…
The American colonists controlled a thin strip of land on the…	The Americans controlled…
Native Americans were protected from American settlers by…	Native American land was now threatened because…
Slavery existed throughout…	Slavery existed mainly in the…
Most American colonists were loyal to…	Many loyalists were forced to…

2 Use the material in this chapter and Chapter 2 to complete the tasks below:

   a List the short-term effects of the British attempts to raise revenue from the colonists after 1765.

   b Which event, person or development do you think had the most significant consequences for the War of Independence? Explain your answer.

   c Explain, in one paragraph, how the position of slaves after the War of Independence differed from their position after the New York Conspiracy (see page 29).

Writing historically: narrative analysis

When you write a narrative analysis, you need to explain a series of events: their causes and consequences. You need to think about how you express the links between **causes** and **effects**.

Learning outcomes

By the end of this lesson, you will understand how to:

- use conjunctions to link and indicate the relationship between points
- use non-finite verbs to link relevant information or indicate the relationship between points.

Definitions

Coordinating conjunction: a word used to link two clauses of equal importance within a sentence, e.g. 'and', 'but', 'so', 'or', etc.

Subordinate clause: a clause that adds detail to or develops the main clause, linked with a subordinating conjunction such as 'because', 'when', 'if', 'although', etc.

How can I link my points in sentences to show cause and effect?

When explaining complex sequences of events, use coordinating conjunctions to link them in sentences. Look at this exam-style narrative analysis task:

> Write a narrative account analysing the key events of 1770–74 that led to the Intolerable Acts (1774). **(8 marks)**

1. How could you link these three points using just **coordinating** conjunctions, e.g. 'and', 'but', 'so'?

> In March 1770, British soldiers in Boston had killed protesting colonists.
>
> The British authorities wanted to avoid another confrontation.
>
> They moved their soldiers outside the city.

2. You can also use **subordinating** conjunctions to make the relationship between cause and effect clear. For example, linking:

- an explanation: e.g. 'because', 'as', 'in order that', etc.
- a condition: e.g. 'if', 'unless', etc.
- a comparison: e.g. 'although', 'whereas', 'despite', etc.
- a sequence: e.g. 'when', 'as', 'before', 'after', 'until', etc.

Look at these simple, short questions and answers:

a. What reason did the British government give for passing the Tea Act in 1773? *To make tea cheaper and to help the East India Company.*

b. Why did colonial merchants protest against the Tea Act? *They would lose business to the East India Company's agents.*

c. Why did the governor of Massachusetts refuse to send the tea ship *Dartmouth* out of Boston Harbor? *He wanted to show strength and force the colonists to obey the Tea Act.*

d. What caused relations between the British government and colonists to grow even worse? *Some colonists destroyed a shipment of tea worth £10,000.*

3. Rewrite the information in each question and answer as a single sentence. Choose a different type of subordinating conjunction (explanation, condition, comparison and sequence) in each one to express the relationship between cause and effect as clearly as possible.

4. Experiment with different ways of using a subordinating conjunction to link two or more of your sentences into a single sentence.

How can I link my points in other ways?

You can add relevant information and further explanation of cause and effect using **non-finite verbs**. These include facing/faced, determining/determined and worsening/worsened.

Compare these two extracts, written in response to the exam-style question on the previous page:

> *Boston set up a committee of correspondence to strengthen links with other colonies because it was facing the possibility of new British measures.*

Two points are linked using a subordinating conjunction.

> *Faced with the possibility of new British measures, Boston set up a committee of correspondence to strengthen links with other colonies.*

Two points are linked using a non-finite verb.

Look at the two sentences below. How could you link the two points in each one, using a non-finite verb instead of a conjunction? **Hint:** think about how you could use a non-finite form of the highlighted verb.

> *The colonists were determined not to pay taxes imposed by the British government, so they introduced a boycott of British goods.*

> *The situation was worsened in Boston when the protestors started throwing snowballs and shouting at the guards.*

Did you notice?

There are lots of different ways to link points in sentences. Some of them make the relationship between points more clearly than others.

5. Choose **one** of the sentences above. Experiment with rewriting it in two or three different ways, using different methods to link points. Which version expresses the relationship most clearly and fluently?

Improving an answer

Now look at this paragraph from the beginning of one student's response to the exam-style narrative analysis task on the previous page:

> *Boston was headquarters of the customs commissioners. Mobs gathered outside the customs house to attack the officials. The colonists did not want to pay the duties imposed by the Revenue Act. On 5 March 1770, a mob was throwing snowballs and icicles at the guards. One guard fell to the ground. He fired at the protestors. Other soldiers thought they had been ordered to fire. They shot into the crowd and several colonists were killed.*

6. Try rewriting this paragraph, using conjunctions and non-finite verbs to make the sequence of events, and the relationship between cause and effect, clear.

7. Continue the response above with a second paragraph explaining how the situation developed. Use conjunctions and non-finite verbs to make clear connections between causes and effects.

Writing analytical narrative

The difference between a story and a narrative account that analyses

Paper 2, Question 2 will ask you to 'Write a narrative account analysing…' (see page 102 in *Preparing for your exams*). You are not being asked to tell a story in the examination; you are being asked to explain how events led to an outcome. This means showing that the events are a series of happenings that have links between them. To do this, you must show that:

- events are prompted by something
- these events react with other events (or perhaps they react with existing circumstances)
- consequences follow from them.

Showing links like these is what turns a story into 'an account that analyses'.

Narratives for young children are always stories; they deal with events and descriptions. For example, many versions of the adventures of Toad of Toad Hall, originally described in the children's book *The Wind in the Willows*, have been published. These narratives show how Toad got himself into a number of scrapes. One episode describes his fixation with acquiring a fast car, his theft of one, his arrest for dangerous driving and his subsequent trial and imprisonment.

Here are some extracts from *The Wind in the Willows*.

Toad steals a motor car

Toad had a passion for cars. He saw a car in the middle of the yard, quite unattended. Toad walked slowly round it. 'I wonder,' he said to himself, 'if this car starts easily.' Next moment he was turning the starting handle. Then he heard the sound of the engine and, as if in a dream, he found himself in the driver's seat. He drove the car out through the archway and the car leapt forward through the open country...

This extract has the first important ingredient of narrative: sequence – putting events in the right order. Words and phrases like 'next moment' and 'then' show the sequence. However, it lacks the analytical links between events. In this case, key links could be built around phrases such as 'because', 'in order to' or 'as a result of this'.

For example:

Toad saw the car parked in the middle of the yard. Because there was no one with it, he took the opportunity to have a good look at it. He even gave the starting handle a turn in order to see how easily it started. It started easily, but the sound of the engine affected Toad so much that his old passion for cars resurfaced and his urge to drive the car increased to such an extent that it became irresistible. As a result, as if in a dream, he found himself in the driver's seat...

The analytical narrative, as well as linking events, also makes clear what followed on from them – what difference they made. It uses process words and phrases that show something was happening. In this example, the process words and phrases are 'affected', 'resurfaced', 'increased' and 'became'.

Activities ?

1. Choose a story that you know well – or think of a plot for a story of your own.

2. Select up to eight key events in the story and list them in a sequence. Ideally, these events should be from the beginning, middle and end of the story (if two things happen at the same time you can list them together). Create a flow chart with arrows from one event to the next in the sequence. Label your arrows with links chosen from the chain of linkages (see Figure 1).

3. Write a narrative account analysing the key events of your story. Use the links and at least five process words. Choose them from the process word case (see Figure 2) or use others of your own. Remember that events can combine with long-standing feelings or circumstances as part of the narrative (for example, Toad's passion for motorcars).

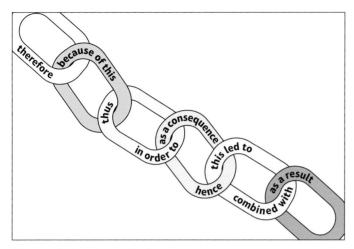

Figure 1 The chain of linkages

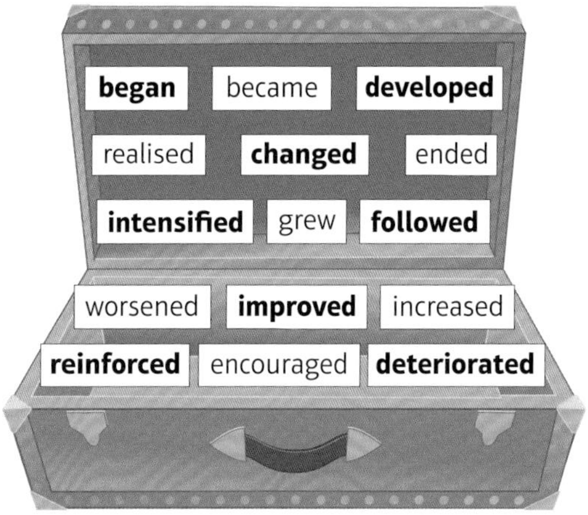

Figure 2 Process word case

Writing historical accounts analysing…

You may be asked to write an account that analyses the key events which led to something, or the key events of a crisis, or the way in which something developed. This example has shown the skills you will need to write a good historical account. As you prepare for your examination, you should practise by:

- selecting key events
- sequencing them
- linking them into a process that explains an outcome.

As you study the events of British America, 1713–83, note the linking phrases and process words the author has used in this book. You should add them to your own lists. When you create your own analytical historical narratives, try to make use of both linking phrases and process vocabulary.

Activities	?

Study the timeline on page 49. You can use the events from it to help you to answer the following question: Write a narrative account analysing the key events of King George's War, 1744–48.

1 With a partner, write the events on pieces of card, without their dates, and then:

   a practise sequencing them correctly

   b agree on another one or two events you could choose to include in your account and any events you could remove

   c identify an instance where long-standing circumstances (or attitudes) were involved as events unfolded.

2 Working individually, write your own narrative account, with linkages and showing a process. Focus on what it is you are explaining and choose process words which relate to, e.g. the setting up of different organisations and alliances.

3 Either swap accounts with a partner or check your own account. Highlight linkages in yellow and process words in green. You can use the same words more than once, but aim to have at least five green and five yellow highlights. See if using more 'process words' improves your account even more.

You are now ready to complete your exam question. Remember to use **SSLaP**.

- **S**elect key events and developments.
- **S**equence them in the right order.
- **L**ink them, **a**nd

- Show the **P**rocess that led to the outcome of your analytical narrative.

Preparing for your GCSE Paper 2 exam

Paper 2 overview

Your Paper 2 is in two sections that examine the Period Study and British Depth Study. They each count for 20% of your History assessment. The questions on British America are the Period Study and are in Section A of the exam paper. You should use just under half the time allowed for Paper 2 to write your answers to Section A. This will give a few moments for checking your answers at the end of Section B.

History Paper 2	Period Study and British Depth Study			Time 1 hour 45 mins
Section A	Period Study	Answer 3 questions	32 marks	50 mins
Section B	Depth Options B1 or B2	Answer 3 questions	32 marks	55 mins

Period Study Option 22/23: British America, 1713–83: empire and revolution

You will answer Questions 1, 2 and 3.

1 Explain two consequences of... (2 x 4 marks)

Allow 10 minutes to write your answer. Write about each consequence. You are given just over half a page for each. Use this as a guide to answer length. You should keep the answer brief and not try to add more information on extra lines. This will make sure you allow enough time for later questions worth more marks. Make sure you focus on consequence: 'as a result', 'as a consequence' and 'the effect was' are useful phrases to use.

2 Write a narrative account analysing... (8 marks)

This question asks you to write a narrative explaining how events led to an outcome. Allow 15 minutes to write your answer. You are given two information points as prompts to help you. You do not have to use the prompts and you will not lose marks by leaving them out. Always remember to add in a new point of your own as well. Higher marks are gained by adding in a point extra to the prompts. You will be given at least two pages of lines in the answer booklet for your answer. This does not mean you should try to fill all the space. The front page of the exam paper tells you 'there may be more space than you need'. Aim to write an organised answer, putting events in the right order and showing how one connected to the next. Your narrative should have a clear beginning, middle and end.

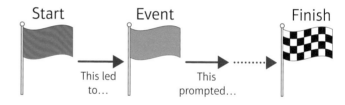

3 Explain two of the following... (2 x 8 marks)

This question is worth half your marks for the whole Period Study. Make sure you keep 25 minutes of the exam time to answer this. The question asks you to explain the importance of events and developments. You have a choice of two out of three. Take time to make the choice. Before you decide, be clear what you have to explain: the question is always worded as 'The importance of... for...' It is a good idea during revision to practise identifying the importance of key events for something: What did they affect or lead to? Ask yourself: 'What difference did they make to it?' or 'Why did they matter?' Be clear about your reasons for saying something is important.

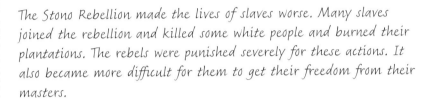

Explain **two** consequences of the Stono Rebellion (1739). **(8 marks)**

Average answer

The Stono Rebellion made the lives of slaves worse. Many slaves joined the rebellion and killed some white people and burned their plantations. The rebels were punished severely for these actions. It also became more difficult for them to get their freedom from their masters.

Another consequence was that colonists became more afraid of their slaves. Lots of slaves had joined the rebellion as the slaves marched through the countryside. After the rebellion, masters were told to look after their slaves better.

A very general consequence is identified here. There is support given, but it shows limited knowledge of the topic. It could be improved with some specific factual detail that focuses on the consequence.

A second consequence is identified, but again the supporting evidence is too generalised. It could be improved with more explanation focused on the impact of the event.

Verdict

This is an average answer because:
- it identifies two consequences
- it supports each consequence with some general information about the topic.

Use the feedback to rewrite this answer, making as many improvements as you can.

Paper 2, Question 1

Explain **two** consequences of the Stono Rebellion (1739). **(8 marks)**

Exam tip

This question wants you to explain the results of something. What difference did it make? Use phrases such as 'as a result' or 'the effect of this was'.

Strong answer

One consequence of the Stono Rebellion was that it increased the restrictions placed on slaves in South Carolina. The effect of the rebellion was that white colonists thought slaves had too much freedom, which had helped them to organise the rebellion. As a result, the Negro Act was passed in 1740, which fined masters who could not control their slaves and removed a master's right to grant his slaves their freedom. This meant that slaves would now find it more difficult to gain their freedom, either by legal means or through rebellion.

A consequence is clearly identified and is supported by specific factual detail. The final sentence clearly explains the consequence identified at the start of the paragraph.

Another consequence was that the colonists tried to reduce the chance that another slave rebellion would succeed. The colonists were afraid of another uprising, which meant they tried to limit the increase in the slave population. As a consequence, a high tax was placed on slaves bought from abroad. The effect of this was to decrease the number of newly imported slaves and increase the number of European migrants. This meant there would be fewer slaves to join a rebellion and more colonists who could stop one.

A second consequence is identified and supported by specific factual detail. Key phrases like 'as a consequence' and 'the effect of this' help to keep the explanation focused on consequence.

Verdict

This is a strong answer because:
- it identifies two different consequences
- it supports each consequence with specific factual detail
- the explanation focuses on consequence.

Paper 2, Question 2

Write a narrative account analysing the key events of 1758–60 that led to the French surrender.

You may use the following in your answer:

- the French abandon Fort Duquesne (1758)

- the capture of Montreal (1760).

You **must** also use information of your own. **(8 marks)**

Average answer

Before 1758, the British had suffered defeats and had lost important forts. From 1758 onwards, they began to achieve victories. They recaptured the fort at Louisbourg, which they had given back at the end of the last war. Then they forced the French to abandon Fort Duquesne in November 1758 and they built Fort Pitt on the same site. After this, they moved the fight to Canada. From June to September 1759, General Wolfe besieged Quebec. He fired at the city and cut off their supplies. He then got into a battle with the French and managed to capture Quebec from them.

At the same time, two other generals took other important forts in Canada. By 1760, the British were ready to end the war. The British forces under General Amherst attacked Montreal. The French surrendered the city and gave up their war efforts in America.

The answer mentions events from before 1758, which cannot be rewarded. Instead, it should explain what the capture of Louisbourg led to.

The answer includes an additional point about the campaign in Quebec, but more needs to be explained about the shift from the Ohio Country to Canada.

The answer is organised, as it is in chronological order. It could be improved by explaining the links between each of the relevant events listed in the answer.

Verdict

This is an average answer because:

- the information is mostly relevant, completely accurate and in the correct chronological order

- it lacks the explanatory links to show the connections between events

- it does not explain why the events led to the French surrender.

Use the feedback to rewrite this answer, making as many improvements as you can.

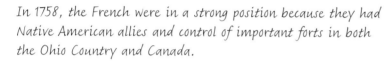

Paper 2, Question 2

Write a narrative account analysing the key events of 1758–60 that led to the French surrender.

You may use the following in your answer:

- the French abandon Fort Duquesne (1758)

- the capture of Montreal (1760).

You **must** also use information of your own. **(8 marks)**

Exam tip

Include key events and the links between them to give an explained account. Cover the years given in the question and remember to add at least one of your own points.

Strong answer

In 1758, the French were in a strong position because they had Native American allies and control of important forts in both the Ohio Country and Canada.

The answer begins well, as it establishes the situation in 1758. This provides a starting point for an explanation of how the French position is weakened by each development.

However, in 1758 their fortunes began to change because the American colonists received more help from the new British prime minister, William Pitt. This enabled them to achieve an important victory in July 1758 and recapture the French fort at Louisbourg, which cut off their supply route. The situation worsened for the French when the British captured Fort Frontenac, in August 1758, which contained most of their remaining supplies. This defeat made the French look weak, so their allies, the Native Americans, abandoned them.

The answer links the events together with connectives and information that shows an understanding of changing relationships and situations.

Faced with limited supplies, and the loss of their allies, the French burnt down Fort Duquesne so that the British could not capture it. Instead, the British built Fort Pitt on the same site, which secured their control of the Ohio Country. The British were now free to focus on Canada. From June to September 1759, General Wolfe successfully laid siege to Quebec.

An additional point is added about the siege of Quebec, which helps to explain the successful attack on Montreal a year later.

This provided a distraction, which General Johnson used to help capture the French fort at Niagara and General Amherst used to capture two other forts. These victories were achieved quickly because the Native Americans were now helping the British. These quick victories meant that, by September 1760, all the British forces were free to combine and take the last French city. As a result, they took Montreal on 7 September. Faced with the loss of their forts, settlements and allies, the French had no choice but to surrender.

The concluding statement builds on the explanation that has been developed throughout the answer.

Verdict

This is a strong answer because:

- the information is relevant, accurate and shows good understanding of the events

- it gives explanatory links to show the connections between events

- it has a coherent line of reasoning to show why the events led to the French surrender.

Paper 2, Question 3

Explain **two** of the following:
* The importance of the Piracy Act (1717) for the suppression of piracy. **(8 marks)**
* The importance of King George's War (1744–48) for relations between the British colonists and the Native Americans. **(8 marks)**
* The importance of the Declaration of Independence (1776) for slavery in the United States of America. **(8 marks)**

One event is demonstrated below as an example, but your answer would need to include a discussion of a **second** event as well.

Exam tip

You are not asked to describe the event, but to explain its importance. Think about its significance. What did it lead to or change? What difference did it make?

Average answer

Before the Declaration of Independence slaves could only get their freedom if they asked for permission from their master, or the colonial assembly gave it to them. They did not have much freedom. They could not travel or sell things and they were not allowed to gather in large groups.

The answer provides too much information about the situation before the Declaration of Independence. The opening statement could be improved by stating a reason why it was important instead.

In 1776, the Declaration of Independence said that 'all men are created equal'. Afterwards some slaves in the northern colonies tried to get their freedom. However, in the southern colonies slaves were too important for the tobacco and rice plantations. They did not get their freedom and many ran away from their masters instead.

A valid point that slaves tried to get their freedom after the Declaration was signed. It would be better to explain how the Declaration affected this development.

Verdict

This is an average answer because:
* the information about the Declaration of Independence and the actions of slaves is accurate, showing some knowledge and understanding of the period
* it does not explain importance enough to be a strong answer
* there is some development of points, but the line of reasoning is not clear.

Use the feedback to rewrite this answer, making as many improvements as you can.

Paper 2, Question 3

Explain **two** of the following:

- The importance of the Piracy Act (1717) for the suppression of piracy. **(8 marks)**

- The importance of King George's War (1744–48) for relations between the British colonists and the Native Americans. **(8 marks)**

- The importance of the Declaration of Independence (1776) for slavery in the United States of America. **(8 marks)**

One event is demonstrated below as an example, but your answer would need to include a discussion of a **second** event as well.

Exam tip

You are not asked to describe the event, but to explain its importance. Think about its significance. What did it lead to or change? What difference did it make?

Strong answer

The Declaration of Independence was important because it influenced the constitutions of the northern states. In 1780, the constitution that was written in Massachusetts said that 'all men are born free and equal'. This encouraged slaves in Massachusetts to use the courts to sue for their freedom. For example, Quok Walker successfully gained his freedom using this method. Other slaves soon followed his example. As well as encouraging slave action, the Declaration also affected the actions of state governments in the north. For example, in 1780, Pennsylvania began to introduce abolition laws. It took until 1799 for states like New York to follow their example, but slavery was beginning to come to an end in the north.

So, the importance of the Declaration was that it kick-started the abolition movement in the north, but it did not have the same impact on the southern states. These states depended on slaves for tobacco and rice production, which meant they were not provided with a way to get their freedom. As a result, many slaves realised that the Declaration would not bring them freedom and 80,000 escaped during the war that followed. However, many more remained. So the declaration was important in increasing the difference between the north and the south as slavery began to shift from being a national to a southern feature of life in the USA.

The importance of the Declaration in leading to new opportunities for freedom in the northern states is explained with specific information.

The importance of the Declaration for the future of slaves in the southern colonies is clearly explained. The concluding statement emphasises its impact on the bigger picture.

Verdict

This is a strong answer because:

- accurate information is included, showing good knowledge and understanding of the impact in both the northern and southern states

- the explanation shows analysis of importance

- the line of reasoning is coherent and well structured.

Answers to recall quiz questions

Chapter 1

1 Germans, Scots-Irish, English
2 10%
3 Edward Teach, known as Blackbeard
4 Answers could include pardons; the Piracy Act (1717); the use of the Royal Navy
5 70,000
6 1713
7 South Carolina
8 9 September 1739
9 Answers could include burglary; arson; conspiracy
10 Molasses Act

Chapter 2

1 The Great Awakening
2 Boston
3 Answers could include the Union Fire Company; street paving; improvements to Philadelphia's watchmen; set up the Academy; helped set up the city hospital in Philadelphia
4 June 1745
5 Ohio Country
6 Answers could include the British national debt increased; Britain controls the fur trade; the Sugar Act was introduced
7 Treaty of Paris, 1763
8 French
9 3 pence
10 1763

Chapter 3

1 Sons of Liberty
2 Five
3 Boston Tea Party
4 Second Continental Congress
5 Thomas Jefferson
6 France
7 Yorktown
8 Treaty of Paris, 1783
9 Massachusetts
10 60,000

Index

Key terms are capitalised initially, in bold type with an asterisk.

Acknowledgements

The publisher would like to thank the following for their kind permission to reproduce their photographs: (Key: b-bottom; c-centre; l-left; r-right; t-top)

akg-images Ltd: De Agostini Picture Lib 80, 81; **Alamy Images:** Classic Stock 4, 38, 46, North Wind Picture Archives 8, 16, 22, 59, Pictorial Press Ltd 14, 73; **Bridgeman Art Library Ltd:** © Collection of the New-York Historical Society, USA 31, Ickworth House, Suffolk, UK / National Trust Photographic Library 6tc, 52, Museum of Fine Arts, Boston, Massachusetts, USA / Gift of Howland S. Warren 68, 86, Private Collection / Peter Newark American Pictures 43, Private Collection / Photo © Christie's Images 85, Private Collection / Photo © Gavin Graham Gallery, London, UK 7, 15; **Getty Images:** Ann Ronan Pictures / Print Collector 21, Buyenlarge 55, John Collet 6bc, 40, Print Collector 34; **Library and Archives Canada:** 95; **Science Source:** 51

Cover images: *Front:* **Bridgeman Art Library Ltd:** Sterling and Francine Clark Art Institute, Williamstown, Massachusetts, USA.

All other images © Pearson Education

We are grateful to the following for permission to reproduce copyright material:

Extract in Source E on page 16 adapted from *The Republic of Pirates: Being the true and surprising story of the Caribbean pirates and the man who brought them down*, Pan Books (Woodard, C. 2007) pp.173–174; Extract in Interpretation 1 on page 28 from *Slavery and the British Empire: From Africa to America*, Oxford University Press (Morgan, K., 2007) p.141; Extract in Interpretation 2 on page 33 from *Colonial America: A History to 1763* by Middleton, Richard; Lombard, Anne S. Reproduced with permission of Wiley-Blackwell in the format Book via Copyright Clearance Center; Extract in Source B on page 40 AND Interpretation 1 on page 41 from *The American Pageant* by Bailey, Thomas Andrew; Cohen, Lizabeth; Kennedy, David M. Reproduced with permission of Houghton Mifflin Company (School Division) in the format Republish in a book via Copyright Clearance Center; Extract in Interpretation 2 on page 43 from *American Colonies* by Alan Taylor, copyright © 2001 by Alan Taylor. Used by permission of Viking Books, an imprint of Penguin Publishing Group, a division of Penguin Random House LLC; Extract in Interpretation 1 on page 63 from *The Scratch of a Pen 1763 and the Transformation of North America*, Oxford University Press (Colin Calloway, 2006) p.76, By permission of Oxford University Press, USA; Extract in Interpretation 1 on page 77 adapted from *Revolutionary America, 1763–1815: A Political History* by Cogliano, Francis. Reproduced with permission of Taylor & Francis Group LLC in the format Book via Copyright Clearance Center; Extract in Source D on page 81 from *The American Pageant* by Bailey, Thomas Andrew; Cohen, Lizabeth; Kennedy, David M. Reproduced with permission of Houghton Mifflin Company (School Division) in the format Republish in a book via Copyright Clearance Center; Extract in Interpretation 1 on page 83 from *America, Empire of Liberty* by David Reynolds (Allen Lane, 2009). Copyright © David Reynolds, 2009 and Perseus Books Group with permission.